MY CAR WAS A

Jowett

To Roger,
with very best wishes

from Noel Stokoe

MY CAR WAS A

Jowett

Noel Stokoe

TEMPUS

I wonder if this family is having a day at the races, or similar event, in their fabric saloon? This is in fact a postcard I bought from a dealer over the Internet! It was such a nice picture, so it seemed a shame not to use it!

First published 2003

Tempus Publishing Limited
The Mill, Brimscombe Port,
Stroud, Gloucestershire, GL5 2QG

British Library Cataloguing in Publication Data.
A catalogue record for this book is available from the British Library.

ISBN 0 7524 2796 2

typesetting and origination by Tempus Publishing Limited
printed in great britain by Midway Colour Print, Wiltshire

Contents

A Jowett Car Club rally in the late 1920s, I can count over fifty vintage Jowetts in the picture! The venue was in Knaresborough, North Yorkshire.

Acknowledgements

First and foremost, I would like to thank the 110 people who have taken the trouble to write to me, telling me about the Jowetts that they once owned. I value all these contributions, as without them there would have been no book!

I would also like to thank my family: firstly my wife Jane, who puts up with this Jowett obsession of mine, which is slowly taking over the house; and my children, Jonathan, Jessica and Ben, who have helped me with the typing. Also to Jan Rochester, who works with Jonathan – she made the mistake of saying she had time on her hands, so she was also roped in to do some typing! My thanks also go to Eden Lindsay and Edmund Nankivell, who have copied several of the photographs in the book on my behalf.

Special thanks should also go to Campbell McCutcheon at Tempus Publishing for sanctioning this book, and my previous one. Without his support, these books would not have been possible.

Introduction

Ever since the first prototype Jowett car was built by Ben and William Jowett in 1906 there has been a special bond between Jowett owners, a real sense of camaraderie. Jowett production started in 1910 and forty-eight cars were built prior to the cessation of production due to the First World War effort. Production started again in full swing in April 1920 at a new factory in Idle, which at that time was just outside Bradford. This would be the home of Jowett Cars until the end of production in 1954.

The Jowett was a cheap and robust vehicle, which brought car ownership – which in the 1920s was still very much a rich man's hobby – to working people. Now ordinary people were able to get out and about into the country for work and pleasure.

It was clear that many of the people buying Jowetts in the 1920s were buying a car for the first time, and were understandably very proud of them. The Jowett brothers were very keen to build camaraderie among Jowett owners. Various Jowett clubs were set up in the early 1920s, notably The Northern Jowett Car Club in 1922 followed by The Southern Jowett Car Club in 1923. Other local clubs were set up after these two. After the war, only The Southern Jowett Car Club survived, and this then catered for the whole country. In 1964 the word 'Southern' was dropped to create The Jowett Car Club of today. We can therefore trace our origins back to 1923, making us the oldest one-make car club in the world.

The *Drivers Handbook*, which was published through the 1920s and 1930s, would echo the Jowett-owners feeling of camaraderie, having a three-page article headed 'Road and Car Camaraderie'. I think this is an excellent read, so I am reproducing it in its entirety overleaf, as it will get you in the mood for the selection of letters from owners of pre-war Jowetts, which follow.

I have called this first chapter on pre-war ownership 'This Freedom!' – a reference to one of the wonderful sales brochures from the 1920s of the same name. Like the handbook, it extols the virtues of Jowett ownership, and some of the text from this brochure is given on the next page.

I have been the press officer and librarian of The Jowett Car Club since 1985, and also the press officer of The Jupiter Owners Auto Club for around ten years. These letters are all from people who have contacted me after seeing my requests for Jowett information, asking for ex-Jowett owners to contact me with their reminiscences. These requests have been published in various publications over the years. My most notable successes so far have been in the *Daily Telegraph, Saga* magazine, *Yorkshire Life, Mature Tymes, The Dalesman*, numerous local newspapers plus the 'classic car' magazines.

If you are reading this and are an ex-Jowett owner, and have not been in touch with me before, I would like to hear from you! Contact me at:

16 Eskdaleside, Sleights, Whitby, North Yorkshire, YO22 5EP

Noel Stokoe

THIS FREEDOM

The Seven Horses

IS there a mystery in seven? It is the perfect number, you know, accounted so in history and religion. We claim no mystery for the Jowett Seven. Seventeen years' experience, following four years' experiment, leave little opportunity for illusions. The fact is, we never had any. But *you* had. Not that we can blame you. Were you not led to believe that low-powered cars were useless, by the very men who should have known better? They took the line of least resistance and piled on the power to obtain the performance. We cut down the weight.

Dr. Benjamin Jowett, that famous Master of Balliol, was tried for heresy in 1860. He was acquitted.

This remarkable product of a later Jowett was regarded as heretic, and opposed with all the vigour of a former fanatical generation. To-day it stands acquitted, proved to be founder of the economy motoring movement, the Master of the college of motoring economy. But it is more. In the course of time our concentrated efforts have built into our car a personality, a "soul" if you will, and in addition to satisfying every essential to motoring economy it converts every owner into an enthusiast.

The very title of this book (Sir, this is not a Catalogue!) conveys to you that we sell you more than a car. What is a Car? A means to an end, perhaps, but a Jowett is something more. A railway train is a means to an end—but what a means—and what an end! A ticket-punching crowded soulless vehicle, to be endured because at the end you may find pleasure, or must find business.

The Jowett alters all this. It is the Car that spells FREEDOM. As you read these pages this freedom will be made ever more apparent; and in case you think business should come before pleasure, we hasten to remind you that the aim of all business, as we see it, is to provide those pleasurable health-giving relaxations without which business and life become drudgery. ·

SEVEN horses cost some corn! but the seven horse-power of the Jowett costs less than tram fare. That is why the Jowett means "freedom" for busy people in every walk of life. It removes the *walk* and enriches life.

John Smith at the directors' table, whose pliant brain daily throws the shuttle of commerce to and fro, must be swiftly on the spot, urgently on the heels of opportunity. Not for him to stamp impatiently at the tram-stop—there's little prestige in a tram-ticket, and none in a queue—yet the Jowett costs him no more than a tram-ticket.

The doctor, conservator of human health, a crusader against disease. Service, he stands for. No strident luxury car for him. Him the Jowett serves well. As easily up the winding by-road to the distant farm as to the suburban villa. Its low running cost can hardly deplete his well-earned fee.

But John Smith at the directors' table (or the doctor by the sick bed), or any plain John Smith, is "daddy" on the nursery floor. And when work is over—there's freedom waiting on the threshold. Freedom for him, for her, for them.

1 This Freedom
Pre-war Jowett ownership

Road and Car Camaraderie
Taken from the Drivers Handbook, issued in the 1920s

YOU are now an initiate to the freedom of the open road. I do not presume to lecture you, but as you have entered into a glorious heritage, perhaps you will allow an 'old hand' to offer a few suggestions as to how best to use that freedom for your own greater pleasure and safety, as well as that of other users of the King's Highway, who may not be so conscientious as you are.

That, however, should not affect you, because you will use the road, as you know is right, and ignore anyone who does not understand the ethics of these things.

Years ago, there was a wonderful camaraderie of the road, and almost every motorist exercised those little functions of politeness, willing assistance, and (sometimes) self-denial in order to assist in the general well-being of all parties. For instance, even today an old motorist descending a hill will give as wide a berth as possible to a motorist climbing. It's no end of a help to him, because his car may be just at the 'last gasp', and, if baulked, it might mean a restart under awkward conditions.

Again, a knight of the road will never toot-toot violently for permission to roar past another on a hill, unless he is quite sure that his less fortunate fellow will not be inconvenienced and perhaps flustered at a time when he is coaxing his rather indifferent engine up the big hill.

I might add to these examples many others and propose to give one or two more, but I would like to say at this stage, that, having bought a Jowett car, you will particularly apply the examples just quoted, because you own a car which can climb severe hills with such consummate ease that you will be more than pleased to give the other man all the room he desires – and more.

This camaraderie of the road is practised by the large majority of Jowett owners. For instance, you will note that another Jowett owner will almost always salute you as he passes.

He will never pass you standing on the roadside without assuring himself you are not in need of help. As a matter of fact, a very old friend of the writer was recently in trouble with his big limousine. He assured me that not a single Jowett car passed him without the owner offering assistance, and one even offered to tow him to the nearest town – with his little Jowett! Only Jowett owners applied the principles of road camaraderie. Will you carry on this good work? Your Jowett will engender the enthusiasm, the desire, because it will make itself a real 'pal' to you, and, doing so, will make you one of this great band of 'knights of the road'.

This is not sloppy sentimentality – it's cold fact.

This enthusiasm has been the means of forming no less than three Jowett Car Social Clubs, and a host of unofficial little clubs, or bands of Jowett Car owners, in various parts of the country.

And now for one or two more examples of applied camaraderie.

Never pass the man in front just because you know you can. One of the most exasperating things is to be passed by a man, and to find that as soon as he is ahead, he perceptibly slows down. Many times on a long run, when averaging a certain previously decided speed, a man has passed me and slowed down just as I have said. Desiring to maintain my average, I have had to re-pass him, whereupon down goes his throttle, and he is by me at a speed I do not desire to maintain, but slows up again and holds me, thus interfering with me in a most undesirable way. Of course, he doesn't realise what he is doing, but you, as a Jowett owner, will not pass the man in front unless you desire to keep ahead and out of his way, will you?

Nor will you travel mile after mile just a few yards behind another car, unless you signal him definitely that you do not desire to pass. Otherwise, he will be continually 'on edge' wondering if you are wanting to pass, or if he is holding you back.

Another little point which may not suggest itself to you at first. If you are driving behind another car at night, put your lights on 'dim'. This avoids shining your headlights into the screen of the man in front – a very disconcerting thing as you will find out when the other fellow does it to you. In any case, you do not need bright lights when travelling behind another car.

I shall not attempt to instruct you in the ordinary rules of the road, as if you do not already understand them, you can obtain the information elsewhere.

Such suggestions as I have given are all concerned with the regaining – rebuilding if you will – of that fine road sense so general in the early days of motoring, and to my certain knowledge and belief, exercised more generally by Jowett owners today than the owners of any other make of car. You will do good to the movement as a whole if you ask your friends to practise these things also.

Finally, if you have not hitherto been a 'roadman', you have quite a lot to learn. The rules of the road should be studied by every new motorist before he drives extensively, as it is usually during his novitiate that he is most apt to contravene these.

At the risk of being dubbed a 'preacher', I would enjoin you to pay some attention to these matters, and you will thereby derive infinitely more pleasure from the use of your car.

A nice 1920s shot of a family out and about in their long-four.

A brew-up at Loch Ness with the 1930 Long Saloon, registered GG 5457, of the Hodge family. When they stopped for picnics etc., Mrs Hodge would sit outside on her passenger seat, which would be taken out for her!

Twas First Love

Our first car – a 1930 Jowett Saloon – we bought in 1948 from a greengrocer in Barrhead – for the sum of £30 (and a pound back for goodwill!) and we were the proud owners – my brother Andrew and I (he paid!) – of a very old and rather the worse for wear Jowett 7 – complete with cabbage leaves and potato shaws in the back, and not quite enough petrol to get us home to Mosspark four miles away (the £1 goodwill spent on petrol to get us home).

We kept 'her' until 1954, when we reluc-tantly parted with her to an enthusiastic friend who 'did her up' with enthusiasm, drove her with enthusiasm and then sold her in a frenzy (just because a wing fell off!).

When we heard he had parted with her at the gates of a scrap yard, we wanted to buy her back – but mother said 'No! That's a ret-rogressive step.' Oh the anguish!

Life with the Jowett was full of incidents and here are some I recall:

★ Learning to drive double-declutching to pass our driving tests, with the examiner more concerned about the car than our efforts – but bravely he sat it out and passed us both.

★ Having to reverse up single-track highland roads that were too steep for two-cylinder cars in first gear.

★ Learning that you could take the bonnet off and climb in beside the engine to do repairs.

★ Learning that 'she' could take five students uphill on one cylinder, with a duff plug in the other one.

Another view of the Hodge family 1930 Long Saloon, taking to the water in the hinterland of Speyside or Strathspey. Note that the nearside headlamp had come adrift when this picture had been taken.

* Using Advance/Retard levers to start her on a cold morning.

* Learning that a fabric body only has a certain life; then you rely on drawing pins.

* Learning that tyres only have a certain life, and that when two layers of canvas appear, its time to take the tyre off and take it to our converted lifeboat and use it as a fender.

* Learning that student grants don't go that far and its time to bring that tyre back from the boat and put it on again.

* A letter from a friend now in Australia reminded me that 'one of her endearing characteristics was an ability to make 360 degree turns on wet cobbled streets' – the tyre went back to the boat.

* Learning to live with the idiosyncrasy of a car that always stalls when it sees a point duty policeman.

★ And when your speedometer oscillates from 3 o'clock to 7 o'clock, get a friend to drive his car in front of you at increments of 10mph and indicate with fingers held out of the driver's window how fast he's going – mark your speedo dial to suit with a felt pen. (Passers-by thought it was rude at 10 and 20mph.)

★ And when you take off the radiator cap and exhaust gases bubble up through the water – you have a leaky cylinder head gasket.

★ Using the advice of an old Carter that radiator leaks are cured by putting a handful of horse manure in the radiator – (hand picked, organically made).

★ And on sharp corners on Highland roads when the wooden floor rubs on the Hardy-Spicer shaft coupling – all you need is a penknife to cut away the floorboards to suit. (The coupling had already been replaced by using a circular piece of conveyer belting!)

★ Was there ever another car where the nearside front door was held shut with a house door security chain?

★ And one windscreen wiper only – the passenger wasn't meant to see out through the snow!

★ It was worth rewiring the car – it meant that the dynamo was charging again – the only trouble was that the headlights had to be on. People kept coming up to tell us 'your headlights are on', so that eventually we put cardboard covers over the lights during daylight hours. Can you think of a dafter answer than 'Well, we keep the headlights on so that the battery gets charged!'

★ And when Andrew took a corner too fast at Inchinnan, hit the kerb (good springs!), the front wheel bounced up, hit the wing and passed the blow to the bar that held the headlamp brackets, which then sheared. So now, wooden brackets were made that held the headlamps to the bar – the trouble was that the headlamps vibrated slowly upwards until they were pointing to the sky! Answer? Easy, thump the brakes and the headlamps returned to the down position. (We nearly had a plane from RAF Leuchars coming in on our beam when leaving St Andrews.)

★ Or the occasion when coming round a single-track road corner and an elegant Rolls-Royce scraped along our mudguard. What a mess (the Rolls-Royce of course!) We had to paint our mudguard again with black anti-fouling paint from the boat.

★ Our fabric body parted occasionally – the roof flew off backwards in a gale on the Loch Tay road – but a rope held it in place until we got to Killin and more drawing pins.

★ In addition, the fabric at the rear parted from the plywood – so a timber strip across the rear held it together – but whose idea was it to 'black' the plank of wood with Mum's 'Zebo' grate polish? Trouble for the push-start person who got back into the car like a black and white minstrel.

★ And then that leaky gasket at the cylinder head. In the morning one of the cylinders was always full of water – easily fixed – remove the spark plug, insert the starting handle, and stand on it. A jet of water would hit the side of the house – it became a challenge to see how high up the wall it went – (rather like little boys playing with their natural toy!) – some rapid cranking while the spark plug was heated along with the breakfast toast and 'hot-handled' to the engine, and away she would go!

* When punctures occurred – which was frequent – to jack up the car a fence post and a boulder off the nearest dyke acted as a 'Pharaoh's Lever' and, if that wasn't enough, a hole was dug in the road to get the spare wheel on.

* And oh, that engine – driving at 40/50mph she would lose power slowly and then pick up at 20mph – repeatedly. Well who would have thought of valve bounce!

* 'She' became the mascot among students at the Royal Technical College when she replaced our Francis Barnett motorbike.

* We travelled the length and breadth of Scotland in those six years – from Moffat in the south to Kingston-on-Spey in the north. She graced many a golf course car park, and many a yachtsman's haven – she quietly endured courting couples in the back seat. Coming ashore at Inverkip in Andrew's boat and finding a note under the only windscreen wiper, proclaiming 'How could I ever forget the car?' and signed by a young lady – Andrew and I looked at each other – Who? Where? You? Me? When? What?!

* We parted with her with great reluctance in 1954.

Yes – 'twas first love for many of us.

Andrew and Robin Hodge, Glasgow

Pre-war Jowett 7 ½

I have what I believe to be an interesting tale regarding a pre-war Jowett 7 that I owned in the 1950s when I was an impecunious young engineer. The car would have been about 1935 vintage and had an open Tourer body with what seemed to be an immense amount of room for a 7hp car. It had a long inlet manifold from a centrally-mounted carburettor, and this manifold was Siamesed with the radiator water connection from the cylinders to the top radiator hose, so that it had a sort of figure '8' cross-section. The land between the inlet air and water passages was somewhat corroded at the flange joint so that it was difficult to make a good joint.

On one occasion, I had been doing some maintenance and had not made a completely tight joint, to the extent that just enough water leaked into the cylinder to create a hydraulic lock, without actually preventing the engine from turning. Once back in action, every time I put my foot down to accelerate, I heard a loud knocking from the engine. My first thought was 'big end', but some dismantling disproved that. Further dismantling revealed a crack about 180 degrees around one cylinder barrel.

I toured the local breakers' yards and managed to find a cylinder barrel off an '8', which had the same bolt locations on the flange, same overall length, and same cylinder head locations. The only problem was that the spigot of the cylinder sleeve, which went into the crankcase, was too big by about a millimetre. I managed to get this machined down in the firm where I worked. Everything was re-assembled and it worked perfectly as a unique Jowett '7 ½'!

Subsequent to that we used to tour North Devon, climbing Porlock, Lynton and Lynmouth Hills, which it did fine, although it did boil climbing Porlock. We also drove to Merthyr Tydfil from Reading to visit some relations, and drove from there to the

THAT'S THE SPIRIT!

JOWETT JOWETT JOWETT JOWETT JOWETT

Such is the enthusiasm engendered by ownership of a Jowett Light Car, that it has resulted in the formation of two Social Clubs, with membership open only to owners of a Jowett.

IN THE NORTH :
The Jowett Light Car and Social Club, with headquarters in Bradford.

IN THE SOUTH :
The Southern Jowett Light Car Club with headquarters in London.

They are not mutual admiration societies, but were formed for the furtherance of the spirit of motoring camaraderie, and the exchange of ideas.

It is interesting to record the fact that most Jowett owners invariaby salute one another as they pass on the road.

Would you not like to become one of this happy band of super-satisfied owners ?

Let us tell you all about the World's Most Economical Car, then decide for yourself whether it is not a wonderful proposition.

PRICE: Completely equipped 2-Seater £168, 4-Seater £192. 7 h.p.   Tax £7.   40 m.p.g. Petrol.   1,500 m.p.g. Oil. 10,000 Miles per set of Tyres.   Write for literature to
JOWETT CARS, LIMITED, IDLE, BRADFORD.

Mumbles and back with a total of four adults and two children aboard.

It gave sterling service, but unfortunately was written off against a Reading Corporation trolley bus when I had to slam on the brakes and swerve to miss a cyclist who came straight out of a side turning without looking. I was really sad when this happened because the car had been such a good servant.

Len Smith, Crowthorne, Berks

Jowett Kestrel

The first car, which I bought when I passed my test in 1956, was a Jowett Kestrel. I lived at Whitley Bay at the time and I had much fun driving it from there to my work in Newcastle-upon-Tyne. It was a large black saloon with a square-ish body and a two-cylinder engine. I paid £35 for it and it felt like a Rolls-Royce!

It was remarkably comfortable and roomy for a two-cylinder car and had the ability to make one feel terribly important, sitting in a high position, as it chugged along.

The only way to start it was by a cranking handle and it was this that led to a parting of the ways. I was trying to start her one winter morning when – yes, you've guessed it – the handle flew back and broke a bone in my arm clean in two! I was unable to drive for a while, and by this time a friend had offered to give me a lift to work regularly. I therefore decided to sell the car, but this proved more difficult than I expected. I eventually let her go for £10 and she is now nothing more than a pleasant memory.

How I wish, looking back, that I had been able to keep the car. The trouble was that I was in lodgings, I had very little money and I had no idea that one day such a car would be a valuable collector's item.

John Farrow, Harpenden

JN 4314

My father, Percy Moore, owned a Jowett Kestrel, registered JN 4314, in the 1930s. I was just a girl at the time, so had no part in its ownership. He was very proud of this car, which gave him and the family a great deal of pleasure. I know he would be 'over the moon' to know that details of his beloved Jowett are now in the club archive.

Miss Audrey Moore, St Albans

FOL 877 – 'The Rattler'

My father, Jack Hodgson, had a black Jowett in 1949/1950. It was the model with the wheel on the back, registration number FOL 877. I don't remember much about it but I'll try to tell you what I can. By the way, we called it 'The Rattler' – because it rattled, of course!

Dad bought The Rattler new from Pickford & Holland of West Road, Crook, County Durham for £30. Pickford & Holland were a brick-making company and the car was used by the manager, work force, old Uncle Tom Cobley and any one who had a driving licence. So, when dad got the chance to buy it, it was in a bit of a state as you may imagine! I remember that the engine block was cracked because it had been out in the frost, (the car, not the block). This was repaired. The other thing of interest was that mam made *all* the leather covers on her trusty treadle sewing machine.

The Rattler continued to be a family 'workhorse' for a good few years; my brother using it, firstly, to learn to drive, then using it for journeys to night school. It was also used for family holidays and day trips. I was taken in it on my honeymoon with my husband in 1952 and also used it to collect my husband, on leave from national service, from Newcastle railway station; a round trip of about forty miles. The Rattler once carried

A lovely 1920s picnic scene with a long-four registered CB 5870. Roads were so quiet in those days, people could stop by the side of the road for a picnic, when the fancy took them!

a gate-legged dining table and four dining chairs (which I'm still using) to my home.

I don't remember much going wrong with the car except dad seemed to be 're-grinding tappets' often. It's the only car I've ever been in which clicked over from 99,999 on to 0. That was quite exciting as you can imagine.

June Luckhurst, Darlington

The car burst into flames . . .

My father had two Jowetts, and he liked them very much. I can remember going round the factory with him. The cars were only 7hp but outstanding at climbing steep gradients – with two adults and four children aboard!

People down south had never seen a Jowett before, and used to crowd round it. I remember a crowd gathered at the foot of Porlock Hill in Somerset to watch us on our way. The road was then unsurfaced, just a dirt road

with a very bad bend at the bottom. We made the climb without difficulty, which I think really impressed the locals, and my father too.

On another occasion, Mr Jowett arrived at my father's unexpectedly and asked him if he would like to try out the car he had brought with him – father agreed, if he could bring his two pals with him. Mr Jowett agreed, and must have been worried when father sorted out two heavy-weights to fill up the car: each was at least sixteen or eighteen stone in weight (including my father). Mr Jowett asked where they should go, and my father suggested Gooseye Brow, which is a really steep climb near Keighley with no chance of taking a run at the hill.

Mr Jowett was driving, my father was next to him, and, halfway up the steepest part, the 'head-lining' in the car burst into flames. Nobody knew that when Mr Jowett had been ready to leave the factory in Bradford he had spotted a dirty mark on the head-lining in the car and had rubbed it with a

17

petrol-soaked cloth. Everyone was quite happy – until my father pulled his pipe from his pocket, lit it, and passed the match over his shoulder to his pal in the back.

That was when the panic started, as the petrol vapour ignited and the flames spread. Mr Jowett said that he knew the car wouldn't start again on that gradient; his passengers couldn't get out of the car quickly enough, but they did make it to the top and everything ended well. I remember Mr Jowett saying that for years this story always featured in the talks he used to give.

Eric Stables, Appleby, Cumbria

RO 9175

In 1931, when I was eighteen, our family decided to buy our first car, which was a 1928 Jowett for which we paid £32. The following describes its main characteristics, or rather those that I can recall.

It was a four-seater Tourer with a fabric hood. The spare wheel was mounted on the offside running board beside the driver. It had bench seats back and front – access to the front seats by a door on the nearside only.

There were two levers on top of the steering wheel, one an ignition advance and retard lever and the other a hand throttle. On the nearside running board was a clamp for a two-gallon petrol can.

The pedal layout was as it has largely remained to this day: left pedal clutch, centre pedal brake, right pedal accelerator. The footbrake operated by an external contracting band closing onto a drum on the transmission shaft. (Imagine the judder when doing an emergency stop!)

The handbrake lever was to the right of the driver and again operated by external contracting brake bands, completely exposed to the weather, onto drums on both rear wheels. This was, in fact, the main brake.

There was no self-starter. The engine had to be cranked after moving the lever on the steering wheel to the retard position. If you forgot, it kicked like a mule! There were three forward gears and reverse. It was a 'crash' gearbox, necessitating double-declutching to change gear.

In the engine compartment here was a cylindrical petrol tank mounted horizontally directly in front of the dashboard, with a pipe feeding petrol to the carburettor by gravity. The engine was a 7hp horizontally-opposed twin. The top speed was just over 50mph. Comfortable cruising speed was around 40mph. In bottom gear, the Jowett would 'go up the side of a house', but with a full load it took only an average hill to reduce it to bottom gear.

We kept the car, registration number RO 9175, for only just over a year and then sold it largely because of its inadequate brakes. In wet weather, if one drove through a large puddle, the brakes almost ceased to function, as neither the footbrake or the handbrake was protected from weather. We sold it for £28. However, during that year, with three passengers (none of us small), I toured Devon and Cornwall for two weeks with no trouble.

Philip Lake, Eastbourne, East Sussex

Twin-cylinder Jowett Tourer

I am seventy-five years of age now and remember as if it were yesterday being taken for a trip to Chertsey by my elder brother, Francis, in his twin-cylinder Jowett Tourer, in 1932. I sat in the 'dickey' seat at the back, and much to my brother's dismay we were 'gonged' by the police on the Chertsey road for making too much noise! The police car was an old Wolseley, the 'gong' being a chromium-plated bell fitted to the front bumper.

The noise we were making was due to the fact that the asbestos tape my brother had wired round the baffle box on the exhaust

A nice shot of a c.1926 Short-2, registered UY 94.

had blown off, as the wire had worked loose. We were lucky and only had a warning from 'the Old Bill', but that was how it was in those days!

Terence Ruinet, West Wittering, Chichester

[*Sadly, Terence died in July 2002, but his widow wanted his letter to appear in the book, and I am most grateful to her. My condolences go out to her and the family. NS*]

PF 1696 and BGW 467

I owned two Jowetts, the first was a 1925 long-four Tourer registered PF 1696, which I owned between September 1948 and the summer of 1949. This had belonged to my uncle, F. John Budgett, who was proprietor of J. Chambers & Son, motor engineers of Redhill, Surrey. I bought it for £30 (I think) and did quite a lot of work on it in Chambers' workshop before driving it to Norfolk. I was in the Navy at the time, serv-

ing with the RN Air Service near Warrington, so the car took me there and around Merseyside with trips over to friends at Ilkley. Then I was drafted to a ship in Portland Harbour, so it took me down there. It was not very suitable for leaving on the jetty while I was away at sea, so I sold it to a civilian acquaintance for £25. I learnt later that the car was scrapped after water entered into the cylinders through a perforated induction pipe.

This car was a year older than me, so often won in an argument, which made driving interesting! It had artillery wheels with no front brakes. There were external contracting brakes on the back hubs and also on the flywheel, but I was advised not to use the latter lest the engine kept on turning and came off its mountings. The three-speed gearbox had no synchromesh and was operated by a lever in a gate by the drivers right leg, as were the rear brakes. There was only one door in the body and that was on

This set of four photographs were taken off as contact prints from old glass negatives. They are a bit of a mystery, as they seem to tell a story. They were rescued from a skip and donated to the club about ten years ago. They show a family out in their Short-2 Jowett, having a picnic. They seem to have a minor accident, and the local policeman is now on the scene to investigate!

the passenger's side. The spare wheel was stowed upright on the running board on the driver's side.

The starter motor gave me some trouble and I often had to rely on the fixed starting handle. With the hood and sidescreens up, a stall on a wet night with a passenger beside you (especially if she was in a long dress) was not very popular, as you struggled to get out of the only door.

The second car was an 8hp 1935 Flying Fox two-seater Tourer, with dickey seat, registered BGW 467, and was a little more respectable! I bought the car from Mr Cassell, an executive with Marks & Spencer, and collected it one lunchtime from outside their head office in Baker Street. I was serving at the RN Barracks Chatham at the time, and the car supported me well in my last bachelor days. It took me all over the South East of England, around Norfolk and once on an overnight trip to Paisley for a friend's wedding. I drove my new bride around North Wales and Yorkshire in it and eventually started to teach her to drive in it, when we moved to Dartmouth. The front seat, however, was fixed and her legs were shorter than mine so she had problems reaching the controls. My father sold the car to a friend in Surrey, after running it for a while himself. This led him to buy a Bradford Utility, but I have no records of it.

I never hankered for a Javelin, as it was somewhat out of my price range at that time. But at a party in Ilkley, I remember meeting and dancing with an attractive girl who said her father worked for Jowetts and had designed the Javelin. You can guess I was impressed! [*This would have to have been Gerald Palmer's daughter, Celia. NS*]

I nearly owned a Bradford Utility. In 1948 my name came to the top of the waiting list at the Jowett agents, Hallens of Cambridge. (No need for salesmanship at that time!) But when interviewed by Mr Hallen, he decided

that I, as a Sub-Lt RN, did not have enough priority, so I was not allowed to buy it! Presumably it went to a Fenland farmer or doctor whose needs were more urgent.

Supplying this information has revived some very happy memories for me.

Robin Budgett, Brockenhurst, Hants

RL 6262

My father was the proud owner of a Jowett, registered RL 6262, when I was a child in the late twenties, early thirties. It was a large four-seater with a convertible hood and 7hp engine. [*Sounds like a long-four, NS*] I can remember we travelled from Truro in Cornwall to Bolton in Lancashire, a distance of 400 miles, on several occasions and usually overnight. My father would also take the car back to the works in Bradford to have all servicing and maintenance work carried out. She was virtually trouble-free and my father used to say if a hill was too steep for the Jowett a stepladder was needed!

Alas I have no knowledge of what happened to the car after my father sold it, before the war – but thank you for giving me the chance to wander down memory lane!

Wendy Heywood née Lightbown, Falmouth, Cornwall

VK 1518

I bought a 7hp Jowett Silverdale, registered VK 1518, in July 1930 for £177, which included tax and insurance. It was paid for out of my twenty-first birthday money. It had four-wheel brakes and the flat-twin engine with detachable cylinder heads. The car was recommended to me, as it was economical to run. Unfortunately it proved very difficult to start; the starter would whiz round uselessly, so the permanently fixed starting handle had to be used.

As it happened, the car managed to find

me a husband; a passer-by who stopped to give me assistance during a minor breakdown in November 1932! With his guidance the car behaved very well, and eventually died of old age.

I am now ninety-three years old and almost blind, having to write by touch. I must be one of the few people left alive who bought a new Jowett over seventy years ago!

Mrs Julia Petrie, Newcastle-upon-Tyne

[*Sadly, Julia died earlier in the year. I therefore send my condolences to her family. NS*]

R 3313

I was born in 1940 at Wallsend, Northumberland, and at that time my parents owned a 1935 Jowett Falcon. It remained in the family for many years, and I guess my sister (born in 1944) and myself grew up with it. It was sold in 1954 to the local Co-op milkman. A lot of my memories of this 7hp car with twin-cylinder engine are still bright. It was originally registered in Northumberland as JR 3313. It was black with spoked wheels and small chrome hubcaps secured with a central screw. The front and back doors were hung on the central pillar, a sunshine roof made of fabric material was fitted, and the windscreen could be opened as it was hinged from the top. At some time water had affected the windscreen glass, and the first couple of inches from the bottom was opaque – a sort of creamy yellow colour. Only one tiny windscreen wiper was provided for the driver.

Access to the boot was from inside the car only; the rear seat backrest was hinged from the top. The spare wheel was fastened externally to the back of the car. I cannot remember if it had semaphore indicators or not, but if there were they never worked, so dad's window was often open for hand sig-

nals. The self-starter never worked either and so the car was always started with the handle. As I became older I remember being shown how to place my thumb behind the handle with the rest of my fingers, so if the engine kicked back, I would not break my thumb. The car had a special spade ignition key, a bit like a small screwdriver. The engine had a distinctive note, and could always be recognised as our car.

After the war ended in 1945 and my dad came home again, the car was regularly used as family transport, although its use was mainly confined to weekends. My dad cycled to his work in the shipyards throughout the 1940s and 1950s, and many cars were used for pleasure only. Most weekends in summer we would travel as a family to the Northumberland coast or country, or occasionally south into Durham. I also remember a summer holiday to Edinburgh in the late 1940s – probably quite a long way to go then with a young family and a 7hp car! Around about this time my dad built his first caravan in the back garden at home, with most of the construction being carried out in the winter months in the spare time he had available. The Jowett pulled the caravan, which seems quite incredible when I look back over this period of my life. I don't think there could have been too much spare power available! We toured for the first year, and then the caravan was permanently sited during the summer months at Beadnell on the Northumberland coast where many good family holidays were enjoyed.

H&G Robinson Ltd were the Jowett agents in the Newcastle-upon-Tyne area and they had a workshop and showrooms on Gosforth High Street (just north of the city and the main A1) and the junction of St Nicholas Avenue. Occasionally our car found its way there, although my dad did most maintenance and repairs himself. Robinson's started selling VW's in the mid-

The c.1934 long-four Tourer owned by Derek Cooper, registered AMC 671; he sold it to a person in the Walton-on-Thames area. This person in turn sold it to the Jowett Car Club for spares in about 1957.

Stop Flirting

As regards married men, this is a needless injunction, for as Ko-ko says in "The Mikado," "Married men never flirt."

We are not speaking of girls, however, but of ideas.

Don't flirt with the idea that new and untried articles will give you the same satisfaction as well-established reputable ones.

Don't flirt with the idea that there is no expense involved in motoring.

Don't flirt with the idea that motoring is absolutely free from trouble.

Stop flirting and get on to solid ground.

The Jowett car has been an accomplished fact for twenty-two years. Had it not been an excellent car, it would have died the death long ago.

Instead of which, we make more and more.

Second point. The Jowett is freer from trouble than any other light car.

Thirdly. It is the light car which costs least to run.

These are the opinions of Jowett owners. Spend your Whitsuntide on a Jowett. It will be the happiest in your life.

Prices from £134. Tax £7

Dunlop Balloons and Stewart Speedometer Standard.

JOWETT CARS LTD., IDLE, BRADFORD.

1950s when Jowett ceased production, and later moved the premises on Kenton Road, Newcastle. Their former premises are now a shopping centre.

After my parents sold their Jowett Falcon in 1954 they had an Austin for a while and then in 1959 bought a ten-year-old Javelin – black and first registered in the County Borough of Sunderland as ABR 669. By this time I had learnt to drive and enjoyed the use of the Javelin with its steering column gear change and handbrake just under the dashboard. Other bits I remember is the neat toolkit in the boot with a place for everything, and access to the spare wheel under the floor obtained by using the wheelbrace. I also recall the radiator grill was hinged for access to the engine and could readily be removed. Some of the door bottoms were showing signs of rust after ten years, and another vulnerable spot was the front part of the rear wings just behind the back doors and the rear part of the front wings, and I practised some early body repair skills on this car.

My dad joined The Southern Jowett Car Club around this time, (I could never understand how it had a name like that, as everything about Jowett's was Northern based) and I still have the badge on my garage wall along with other bits of memorabilia. On into the early sixties and I was keen to pursue a career in either the police force or fire brigade and I borrowed the Javelin on numerous occasions to drive to the locations of tests and interviews. Eventually I joined the fire brigade and enjoyed a happy and fulfilling career for over thirty years.

Malcolm Athey, Newcastle-upon-Tyne

AMC 671

I owned a Jowett Tourer in the early 1950s, registered AMC 671. I used it for a holiday in Salcombe, Devon. It was used for pub transport for seven of us, one for each Horse

Power! I eventually sold the car to a friend in Walton-on-Thames, who also ran it for some time. He sold it to the Jowett Car Club for spares around 1957.

Derek Cooper, Emsworth, Hants

Climbing Post Hill

Here's an interesting story about a Jowett van. There was a bike trail area between Bradford and Leeds called 'Post Hill'. This incident took place in 1947 at a hill climb there. In those days it was difficult to reach the top of the hill, as the motorbikes of the day were not as powerful as they are today. On this particular Sunday there was an ex-major among the spectators watching with interest. He had a Jowett panel van, and threw out a challenge that his Jowett van could climb Post Hill. After the bets were laid, he drove the van to the base of the hill. He then got into the van and reversed it to the top, he then collected his bets from the disbelieving punters!

Sid Drury, Canberra, Australia

FMP 71

I had a Jowett in the 1950s, registered FMP 71 – I understand it was unusual, as it was a four-cylinder model. I owned a garage at the time and took the Jowett in part exchange, keeping it for about a year. It was in very poor condition, especially the engine, which had to be re-bored. New pistons were fitted and the crankshaft was re-ground. After reconditioning the engine it was still using a lot of oil, until I found the crankshaft drain was blocked. After cleaning the drain the engine ran satisfactorily.

One incident I remember was when we were on our way to Liverpool, en route to the TT Races in the Isle of Man for a week. We were going slowly up a steep hill out of Ashbourne, when the passenger door flew

This was a rare four-cylinder Peregrine owned by Trevor and Betty Garratt in the early 1950s, registered FMP 71.

open after hitting a bump in the road. For the rest of the journey the door was tied up with string! As you know, these doors were fastened at the front and hinged at the back, so very worrying if they open when on the move. [*Often referred to as suicide doors! NS*]

One of my customers at the garage in the 1970s was a lady, well into her eighties who ran a Jowett Jupiter sports car. I have been in touch with her granddaughter, but unfortunately she has no details or photos of the car. She remembers being frightened to death by her gran when she took her out in the Jupiter. She sold it to a local man who wrote it off the day after he bought it!

Trevor Garrett, Sutton-on-Sea, Lincolnshire

[*Sadly, Trevor died earlier this the year. His widow, Barbara has requested that I still publish his letter. I am most grateful to her and send my condolences to her and the family. NS*]

Flying Fox, BMA 105

I lived in West Wickham, Kent, and was out cycling with a friend in the Sevenoaks/Westerham area in, I guess, the summer of 1958. Aged twenty-one, I was looking for new excitements in my life and had contemplated getting a car like all my friends had done whilst I was doing my national service – you know, pre-war bangers such as Austins, Morris's, Hillmans, Singers, Triumphs etc. – anything with four wheels, cheap and would at least start!

We were passing through a little village called Toys Hill when we noticed at the rear of a small country garage a very lonely, tatty, sad-looking car with a 'for sale' sign on its windscreen. We stopped to have a look and noticed it was a very upright two-seater, hand-painted black and with what appeared to have a dickey seat and cloth top. An old fellow in overalls, who turned out to be the

The 1934 Flying Fox of Roy Gaved, who bought it in 1958 at the age of twenty-one. At one stage a hard top had been fitted, as it was originally an open Tourer. This is the only example I have seen like this.

garage owner, wandered over and asked us whether we were interested. Yes, says we, how much did he want for it? The reply came 'Fifteen quid, I want to get rid of it because I took it in exchange for a bad debt'! Well bangers were going for about £25 a time then, so we asked him to start it up. She ran, and she looked solid with five reasonable tyres. Because it was not taxed and neither of us had a driving licence, we told him we would go home, get some cash and come back the next day.

Back home I persuaded my dad that this was the real thing and was he prepared to take me out with the cash and tow me home? Well that's what he did the next day. We collected the log book, gave the garage owner the cash, hitched up the towrope and were off. We arrived home safely, without any mishaps, which was perhaps surprising as it had been my first time driving a car, albeit

only being towed! The car was a 1934 two-seater Jowett which I later understood was called a 'Flying Fox'. Typical Jowett two-cylinder horizontally-opposed engine which actually ran reasonably well though rattled a bit.

Having previously driven, stripped down and rebuilt a variety of motorbikes, I was quickly under the bonnet to assess just what I had purchased. The cylinders were cracked at the hydraulic engine mounting flanges. The manifold was badly corroded where it was attached to the cylinders and leaking coolant. The hydraulic mountings were finished and badly rusted. The cylinder bores were worn and the big ends sounded as though they needed attention, but I had a car! None of these were a problem to me! The excitement of youth!

The cylinders went off to Barrimars for welding and then onto a garage to be re-bored with new pistons and rings. A replacement manifold was obtained from a breakers and the hydraulic mountings I decided would be cleaned and modified by using Belville washers as sprung packing in place of the oil. The big ends would have to wait!

All back together again, car taxed and insured, provisional licence obtained and I was on the road. At that time, due to a fuel crisis, a provisional driver was allowed to drive unaccompanied providing he displayed 'L' plates.

So that's how I became a Jowett owner and had some incredible times with that car. On one occasion it took part in a local carnival and carried ten adults on it, all dressed up as devils! The springs must have been good!

I never was able, however, to resolve the problem of leaking manifold gaskets to the cylinder, and subsequently always carried a topped-up watering can in the dickey boot (the dickey seat was missing when I got the car) to replenish the radiator. The coolant used to leak into the cylinders, but only appeared to create minimal problems. I knew when I was in trouble, for one cylinder would cut out, then the routine was to stop, take out a plug, start the engine and pump the water clear, then replace the plug and get under way again! I did this on a number of occasions! I remember doing this one time opposite a bus stop, the looks on the faces of those waiting had to be seen to be believed! On another occasion I was out in the country with a pair of girl twins going up a steep hill. As the car started to stall and was reduced to a walking pace, I yelled to the girls to get out and push! Their combined effort just got me to the top of the hill where I was able to carry out my water-clearing routine, top up the radiator and get under way again to the country pub!

Some months later I was again driving in the countryside along a straight flat valley road. There was a loud mechanical bang from the engine and the car came to a halt. I tried the starter with no luck and in desperation I tried cranking with the starter handle. There were some strange sounds but much to my surprise the engine started. We got back in and gently drove away up a steep hill out of the valley. At the top the car gave another bang and the engine continued on only one cylinder, creating quite a racket. I stopped the engine to investigate but could not determine the problem. When I tried to start again it would not start! So off to the nearest phone box to call dad for a tow!

After stripping the engine later at home it was, as suspected, a broken crankshaft. To this day I do not know how that car continued up the hill after restarting, and how did it then continue to run for a short while on one cylinder with a broken crankshaft?!

So off to the breakers again for a crankshaft, get it re-ground with new big end and main bearings. Rebuild the engine, and once again we were on the road. That car continued running for about another year when the big end bearings ran on the way home from work – almost certainly due to water in the oil. That was it, I had had enough and began looking for another car, I wanted something a little more up-market now – bangers were out! I later called the car-breakers and they towed it away. Even at that stage I felt regrets, for that car had given me a great deal of fun.

Our local car dealer had a metallic grey 1949 Javelin for sale and the price suited me. It was the saloon de luxe with walnut facia and trimmings, leather seats etc. This was a great improvement on the old Jowett!

What a car that was, I felt like royalty driving around in the Javelin. Of all the cars that I have since owned, that was one of the best of three, way ahead of its time in all respects. The other cars I have rated highly were a Citroen GS Club and the Ford Focus that I currently drive. (Interesting that the 'Flying Fox' was originally the 'Focus'!)

The Javelin's paintwork was dull and worn so I decided to respray the body British Racing Green. I took a great deal of time on this work, building up seven coats of paint, rubbing down between each coat. I started on the boot, worked round the nearside over the top, the bonnet and then the driver's side. Unfortunately, having started work on the driver's side I had an accident which wrecked the driver's door and the central pillar! I had it repaired but, after all that work, it had taken the heart out of me, so I quickly finished the respray work and began thinking of selling it to raise cash to buy a house so that I could get married.

This car gave me a great deal of pleasure, comfort and enjoyment. It also, incidentally, gave me the opportunity to attract my wife, who remembers with fondness the 'Javelin'.

Oh how I wish I had both cars now! Every time I see a Jowett on the road or at car shows I view them with envy. The only other 'Flying Fox' that I have ever seen was on the Strand car park at Rye some fifteen years ago. It was identical to mine except that it had its original soft-top.

Roy Gaved, Hastings

Black Prince, EU 4389

I am the ex-owner of a Jowett car. This was a Black Prince model which my father gave me in 1930 at a cost of £100. It looked beautiful with its black fabric body and red moquette interior and red steering wheel. It had red wire-spoked wheels and running boards. There were no windscreen wipers or trafficators and to start the car you pushed a button on the floor. The car was registered EU 4389, which was a Breconshire registration.

The local garage that worked on the car for me used to call it 'the sewing machine'

because of its twin-cylinder engine. I took great pleasure in taking pregnant mums to hospital and fetching them and their babies home. Also using the car for visiting the sick in hospital, even taking pets to the vet! The little Jowett would climb the Welsh hills easily.

I had problems with the starter after a few years – I was told oil had spilt onto it – anyway it did not work, so then I had to use the starting handle. My father was not happy about this, saying 'this was not for a woman', so the car was changed.

A book about our village has just been published and the Jowett car has a mention in it. This is because I was one of the first women to drive in the village. My car gave me and many local folk much pleasure over the years.

I am now ninety-two and am still driving, but not a Jowett of course.

Mrs Nancy Thomas, Crickhowell, Powys

Left in the road

My father was an accountant with the firm Land & Plunkett in Bradford, who seemed to have some involvement with Jowett Cars Ltd. I am not sure if they were auditors to them or to a garage retailing Jowett cars in the area.

He bought a Jowett with a dickey seat in 1933, which we kept for many years, and it still holds many happy memories. The numerous cars that followed never felt quite the same to us.

In those days we lived on the outskirts of Leeds and had a holiday place in Flamborough Head. Travelling there via Garrowby Hill meant my mother and either my sister or I had to alight and walk, as the poor car could not cope with us all plus luggage!

One year we were really adventurous and travelled as far as Minehead, with mother

Right: *L.D. Garrod's father with his 1950 de luxe Javelin. The picture was taken on 9 August 1959. He paid £325 for the car, which had the series 3 engine, which gave him no problems.*

Below: *L.D. Garrod with his 1948 Javelin, which he bought in the 1950s for £250. It had the early engine fitted, with hydraulic tappets, which gave him trouble!*

doing the odd spot of walking! We were camping and it took several days to get there. Because of the possibility of inclement weather, my father purchased a motorcycle sidecar cover to keep us dry in the dickey seat.

I have lots of memories of the car, not least when I was left sitting in the middle of the road when climbing into the dickey seat as the car took off.

Mrs Barbara Hopkins, Devizes, Wiltshire

Early Javelins

I was demobbed from the Army in 1946, having served in the REME, and decided I must have some form of transport. I purchased a 1932 Jowett for £65; it was a 7hp twin-cylinder car with a horizontally-opposed engine. It had a large body, leaf springs front and rear, three-speed gearbox and primitive steering. It was very reliable transport, but not very fast. The only fault I had was the coolant system and inlet manifold, which was one pipe cast in aluminium, water one side and the inlet the other. It was bolted to the top of the cylinder heads, and with engine heat came distortion and water got through into the inlet, causing it to run on one cylinder. This was soon sorted out with a new gasket and some jointing compound.

I ran the car for several years and, during this period, I switched the old three-speed gearbox for a four-speed box, taken from a later model. This required small modifications to get it to fit, but was a big improvement. I well remember my wife helping me to take the engine out and putting it into my wheelbarrow, so I could take it round to my workshop to work on it – happy days!

I had taken a keen interest in the Javelin, and had looked at quite a few; I thought 'I must have one of these when I can afford

one!' This is where I made my first big mistake, as the early models had mechanical problems, as I was soon to find out!

I saw one in a local garage; I was a lorry driver at the time and had driven past. It looked good but smoked a bit. Being a bit of an engineer, I thought I could soon sort it out! I bought it for £250, it was a 1948 model. It still had its original engine with the hydraulic tappets, which were no good from the start. I think Jowetts were the first to fit them, a good idea, but they needed much more done on them. This was the first bad news; it needed a replacement engine, a series three type with the oval web crankshaft. Many of the early engines broke their cranks; a friend of mine broke his. It also needed a new gearbox, so the car was left in the garage while I decided what to do.

I called into Scotts of Colchester, the main Jowett agents, and they had a spare Javelin engine, which I paid £140 for. I decided to buy this and a reconditioned gearbox. These were fitted and I then ran the car for eight years. The car had a good turn of speed for the time, having twin carbs. The other problem I had with the car occurred on very wet roads – water would get into the plug holes, making the car run on three cylinders, and this happened to me several times.

My father also ran a 1950 Javelin, while I was running mine, and we both ended up selling them for £15 each. I wish I still had them now, but we had no room to store them at the time. I am now eighty-one years of age and am still driving; I now run a Rover.

L.D. Garrod, Bures, Suffolk

UK 8720

The first memory I have would be about 1936 (aged six) when a Jowett Tourer came into the family. Previous to this, the family had been transported in the large sidecar attached to an Indian motorcycle. I would imagine that with mother and four growing children, the sidecar seams were bursting. However, I can only picture the Tourer as a long-four but can never remember the hood being down. My main memory of this car was a trip in 1937 after the Coronation to see the decorations in London. In addition to parents and three sisters, we took a large maiden aunt who was travelsick. No wonder the trip sticks in my mind.

Very soon after this trip a newer saloon was introduced, probably due to an increasing amount of water entering through the flimsy celluloid windows and a perishing hood. I find it difficult to pinpoint the model but no doubt you will be able to do so, in spite of the modifications. It was a four-door, long-wheelbase, fabric body.

During the war it was, of course, laid up – in the best way a nine-year-old lad was able to, following instructions from a letter from father in France. He had suddenly disappeared one Sunday night, three months before war was declared, and spirited off to France as part of the BEF advance party as he was in the Reserves. It was not easy trying to jack-up the car in the garage and put blocks of wood or bricks under the axles.

As the war drew to a close, my uncle – who by then had been invalided out of the Army and who, like my father, was a motoring engineer and had joined Newton Oils (Notwen Oils) in Birmingham as transport manager – arrived to prepare the Jowett for

The fabric saloon, registered UK 8720, owned by Revd Ralph Weston's father. This picture was taken on the driveway to his house.

Another shot of Mr Weston's UK 8720.

my father's return. He discovered one cylinder had a crack in the casing – this lad's efforts in draining the water had been either too little or too late. A replacement block was obtained and fitted (this later proved to be of a slightly larger bore which made for a poorer performance than was expected).

However, on return of the soldier father and his resuming of his normal occupation as transport manager for a large Midlands timber importer, the Jowett began to be treated in its rightful way. I seem to remember that the cylinders were bored out and oversize pistons were fitted.

One Friday evening – when precious petrol coupons were being exchanged for the rare liquid (pool petrol) – some spilt over the gravity fed petrol tank and ran onto the hot exhaust, which resulted in a (thank God) small fire, which was quickly put out. So that was the end of the petrol tank under the bonnet. A new tank was fitted between the chassis at the rear of the car, an Autovac

pump was fitted where the old tank had been, and a new bonnet was obtained to replace the fire-damaged one. More modern headlamps were fitted and a rear towing bar. I also think he upgraded the electrical system from six to twelve volts, as a second battery was fitted, in tandem. The old system was not strong enough to power the more powerful lamps and petrol pump. To eke out the petrol, father often added a quantity of paraffin, although much banging and backfiring resulted!

Almost as soon as he returned, my father and I (as gofer) built a trailer, and a large ex-Army tent was purchased so that the whole family could have their first holiday in over eight years. Mother and the girls chose the campsite from the *Camping Club* book; it was in Watchet, Somerset. The trailer was loaded up with the parents, three girls aged eighteen, fourteen and twelve, myself aged sixteen, plus two dogs! It was hard work for 'the little engine with the big pull'! We completed the 140-mile journey with about four stops in ten hours. Not bad in those days when the route went through all the towns on the A38.

The family had to get out and walk up the hill out of Watchet to the farm, but after the holiday, on our way home, the old girl refused halfway up the hill on the Bridgewater side of Watchet. Everybody bailed out, but to no avail, in spite of the pushing ability of the strapping youngsters. Fortunately, a family in a 'modern' Hillman gave us a tow for the last quarter of a mile to the top. The rest of the journey home after this seemed quite uneventful.

My father always felt that the three-speed gearbox was a disadvantage, and at some time he obtained a four-speed one (as far as I know this was from a Jowett). This made the car much more nimble and enabled the revs to be kept up.

Father sank his demob money into a 1930 Austin Light 16, which had been converted into a Civil Defence ambulance during the war. We converted it into a shooting brake and built a 22ft tandem-axle caravan. After the caravan was built, we went on holiday again to Watchet. He felt the 16/6 engine was not quite up to towing this mammoth van so replaced it with a Morris Commercial six-cylinder engine and gearbox, which made it the ideal towing vehicle.

This new vehicle meant that this lad could almost use the Jowett as his own car, but not quite. Father still used the Jowett every day for work, which allowed me the use of it most evenings whilst at university. I also used it to drive down to Somerset on holidays. It seemed that in those days we had more snow and, even though we lived down a narrow country lane, the Jowett was never defeated; mind you, chains did help at times. I often wondered what revs the engine was doing when, on the odd times when the road allowed, we would wind her up to about 55mph, although it felt like 90mph with all the rattles and vibrations!

My father continued to use the old Jowett into the late 1950s; by then I had married and left home. He eventually ran an Austin Somerset and dismantled the Jowett. He ran the Austin for about three years prior to his premature death in 1964.

So much for the Weston Jowett history, they were happy times and I have enjoyed putting these memories down on paper.

Revd Ralph Weston, Tiverton, Devon

Jowetts in the family

My father was very interested in Jowett cars; he was an overseer at the garage of the *News Chronicle* and *Star* (daily and evening papers). When in 1936 my eldest brother wanted a car, my father arranged for him to buy a 1929 Jowett. It was a short chassis saloon with a fabric body.

Having been a driver for about twenty years, my father would have known quite a bit about cars. It cost £20 (I expect my father helped with the funding!) and my brother was very pleased with it. After a tour of Cornwall and Devon the car suffered from gearbox problems, so he exchanged it for a 1928 long-four Tourer.

My brother's Jowett was the first car I ever drove; I had driven his motorcycles from the age of about eleven, but would have been fourteen when I drove the Jowett. No wonder this car went on to have gearbox problems!

My brother tells me that the Jowetts were easy cars to work on; he later went on to buy a Lea Francis. My father died in 1944, but would have been much saddened to learn of the end of Jowett car production in 1954.

Eddie Gardner, New Malden, Surrey

VP 7649

My father bought a Jowett in around 1930, which we had for a number of years up to about 1938. You will have to bear with me as what I am about to tell you is all from memory and I am now seventy-eight years old.

The car was a four-door saloon with a fabric body and a flat-twin engine. It must have been a 1926 to 1928 long saloon, registered VP 7649. We always felt very special in the Jowett, as in those days, if we came towards another Jowett owner, we would salute each other: it was a kind of brotherhood!

My father always started the car with the starting handle as he said the self-starter would drain the battery, it was only a six-volt system. This car never ever gave any trouble and always started on the first pull of the starting handle.

There was no synchromesh in the gear-box, so my father always had to double-declutch when changing gear. By the gear leaver was a smaller leaver which operated the Humfrey-Sandberg free-wheel system. My father said the 'free wheel' saved as much petrol as it used!

I remember my father and uncle fitting new piston rings one Sunday. This seemed to be quite a simple operation as the engine was running again by tea time! The body was brown fabric, with brown rexine upholstery; it was a full five-seater with a large boot accessed by tipping forward the rear seat. Access was also possible from the outside, but the spare wheel had to be removed first. This was used as a 'tuck shop' when my father used the car on scout camps!

It was fitted with artillery wheels, which we regularly painted with black enamel paint; wire wheels came along with later models of Jowett.

We always wished we had the money to buy a new Jowett. I can well remember standing outside Hyde's showroom in Birmingham, the main Jowett agents, look-ing at the latest model inside. This model was the Kestrel, how my mother and I longed and yearned for that car, but it was not to be.

Ivor P. Hill, Pembroke Dock, South Pemb's

Kestrel

I passed my driving test in Leeds in 1952, using the office's Jowett Bradford van, so I was ready to buy my first car. This was a sec-ond-hand Jowett Kestrel, two-cylinder saloon in an olive-green colour. It had a slid-ing roof fitted, and cost me £175.

Up until then my wife and I and two chil-dren had to make the long journey from Dewsbury in Yorkshire to my wife's mother in Ventnor in the Isle of Wight by train. This was an arduous journey, as we had to carry all our luggage as well. Now with this car it was much more enjoyable, even though it took us twelve hours door-to-door. Driving onto the ferry at Portsmouth to Fishbourne or Lymington to Yarmouth was always a real thrill. It meant an early morning start, about 5 o'clock, and with luggage strapped onto the tailboard (which let down to expose the spare wheel), and some inside. We reckoned to reach Blaby in Leicestershire by breakfast time. After that it was time for dinner on a grass verge near Winchester before setting off again for our final destination.

The delights of the Isle of Wight opened out before us as my three weeks' holiday gave us ample time to choose wherever we wanted to go, and find nice spots to have pic-nics, so that we eventually covered most of the island.

Previously, getting out into the Yorkshire countryside entailed long journeys by bus, with limited time when we arrived. With the car we went for miles anywhere we wanted, stopping to picnic at any pleasant spot, and the tailboard served a very useful purpose as a table.

There were some perplexing moments

The Kestrel, registered BPT 155, painted olive green and bought in 1952 by H. Griffin. This picture was taken on 18 July 1952 in the Winchester area.

Another view of the Kestrel owned by H. Griffin; this one was taken at Portsmouth on 26 July 1956.

when going up a steep hill and the radiator began to steam. This happened once when visiting my brother and his wife in Ecclesall, Sheffield. We were going up a hill where they lived, when steam began issuing and we had to stop and ask at a house for water. One day we drove to Haworth but, finding the street was so steeply inclined, we thought that if we went down it we would not be able to climb up again, so we missed out on seeing the historic spots.

Returning from the Isle of Wight on one occasion, en route for Dewsbury, we were not far out of Portsmouth when there was a slight bang and, stopping, I found that the threaded tie rod securing the steering column to the chassis frame had snapped. This was most disconcerting, but the only thing to do was to press on, manipulating the column somehow for the long journey to Dewsbury. Needless to say, I was greatly relieved to get home safely. A new rod was made for me very quickly after that!

After moving to Kenley in Surrey in 1955, we found the car invaluable for driving down to Brighton or Eastbourne for the day and exploring the local countryside.

My mother-in-law had been staying with us in Kenley and, when she was due to go back to the Isle of Wight, we took her as far as Portsmouth for the ferry. Dusk began to fall as we returned, so we switched on the lights and the engine stopped. I switched them off and the engine started again! All we could do then was to pull in behind a hedge and, with the cold night air infiltrating our clothes, we tried rather unsuccessfully to sleep. We remained like this until there was sufficient light for us to start up again, and so we managed to get back to Kenley.

Eventually we part-exchanged it for a second-hand Ford Popular in 1956, but we have a very soft spot in our memories for our dear old Jowett.

John Griffin, Ledbury, Herefordshire

BLN 431

I was already well acquainted with the 1934 Jowett 7hp saloon and vans owned by my father in his business as one of the leading Auto Electrical specialists in the country. At that time I was between college and joining the Royal Navy at the beginning of the war.

I used to help out in the works, as my father had already lost a number of mechanics to the services. I was delighted when I was able to obtain my first driving licence at the end of 1942. I was already able to drive, having learnt to shunt cars and much larger vehicles around within the works etc.

One of the vans was only capable of 45mph because of a restriction of which nobody could understand or correct. On reaching the said speed, the steering had a distinct wobble and the bonnet would shake from side to side. Apart from that it was a super vehicle and travelled many miles on work of national importance.

My aunt was the secretary of the business and owned a 1932 7hp long saloon and she praised every moment of her travels in it. I was not to be outdone and spotted in a local garage a 1935 7hp long saloon, registered BLN 431. It was in a somewhat dilapidated condition, but at a price I could afford at £70.

Joining the service at that time, the car was left in my father's works awaiting my return, which happened at the end of 1946. The priority for me then was to get the car roadworthy and to use it. At the beginning of 1948 the car was on the road, taxed and insured. For the next seven years it gave me immense pleasure and was a great talking point. I covered some 150,000 miles through the length and breadth of the country.

It was not fast, but that did not worry me, in fact it was of great value. Tyres at the time were hard to come by, but a local dealer was able to supply a set of four. These were as supplied to the local industry for their fleet of horse-drawn milk floats! With careful driving a set would cover 40,000 miles.

After about twelve months happy motoring, I decided with a nursing friend to take John, a young lad of seventeen who had been bedridden for three years with poliomyelitis, for a day trip to the Isle of Wight from his home in South London. An early day in autumn of 1949, we loaded up with food etc. for the day, carrying John into the car, settling him in then placing his folding invalid chair on the rear. We set off at the crack of dawn in gorgeous weather. The ferry negotiated and a wonderful day was had. Returning to the ferry in the early evening and about a mile from it, the nearside cylinder developed a miss fire, giving a bumpy ride. To ensure not missing the ferry, I proceeded on and, with the help of the crew, the car was safely brought aboard.

Arriving back in Portsmouth, with assistance, we managed to get back onto the road. I then had to decide whether to call an ambulance or taxi to get John back to London, or risk making the journey back on one cylinder. We all agreed on the second option and we made it back to John's house by midnight. I took the car back to my father's business and left for home, feeling somewhat exhausted. The following day, with time to spare, I took the head off the cylinder to find an exhaust valve with a V-shaped burnt section, and the rest of the inside covered in soot. I cleaned it up, inserted the new valve and replaced the head. The engine started on first touch of the button and once again was purring in the usual Jowett manner. What a wonderful advert for a car, being able to travel sixty miles on one cylinder and a full load!

I got into difficulty one day far from home; a very severe noise occurred in the engine, which brought me to an immediate stop. On close examination I was convinced the crankshaft had broken in two pieces. I could turn the engine over by hand but the clanking sound was awful. I contacted my father, who in turn contacted Jowetts in Idle to ask for their help. They were convinced my diagnosis was wrong, as it could never happen to a Jowett! They said that if the car could be delivered to them for examination, they would supply and fit a new engine, free of charge, if the crankshaft was broken! The car was towed across country to Jowetts, I later collected the car with a new engine fitted! Yes, the crankshaft had broken and the new engine was fitted – Jowetts were true to their word. [*Not bad for a car that was at least sixteen years old … what service! NS*]

I continued to improve the car, and by a heathrobinson arrangement and the use of the induction manifold, fitted a satisfactory heating system that improved the quality of the comfort.

In 1949 I was working for my company from an office based in Dewsbury in Yorkshire. For a New Year's Eve I had been invited, along with about ten others, to a party. The house was in town and on a steep hill which had a T-junction at the bottom into a main road. As was my custom, I had parked the car face-down the hill, handbrake fully on, car in reverse gear and the wheels turned into the kerb.

Party over at 2.00 p.m., leaving the house I noticed the absence of the car, but on looking down the road, a number of people had collected and I joined them, only to find the Jowett in the back room of a chemist's shop. Obviously it had come down the hill, crossed the main road and ploughed into the shop from the back. The police were there, and waiting for a breakdown truck to pull the car from the scene. I confessed to the vehicle being mine, and had no idea as to how it arrived there. Although the car door handle was broken, they would not accept from me that someone must have broken into the car and let the handbrake off.

Kicking Against the Pricks.

The choleric looking gentleman demanded to see our sales representative.

"Good morning," said our representative courteously.

Without replying to this greeting the visitor burst forth somewhat on the following lines.

"I want to test one of your eight horse power cars. I run a twelve horse now but I am not going to pay 25/- per horse power on that, and if the Government think they are going to get extra money out of me for running a car they are mistaken."

We took him for a run during which his cholera abated very materially and in almost pleasant tones he asked what the petrol consumption was. On being told he whistled delightedly and, perhaps, a little incredulously, and for the first time he smiled. "I shall be doing 'em both ways," he chuckled.

He placed his order and took his leave a happier man than when he arrived.

We deliberately chose our headline for this advertisement for there is no getting away from the fact that things have got to be paid for, but to the shrewd observer the fact sticks out a mile that if you want luxurious and yet at the same time, economical motoring you will have to include the Jowett in your calculations when considering your new car. It is the best light car on the market and, withal, there is no other car that will cost you less to run.

If you want a demonstration to prove what we say send us a postcard.

Prices from £159.10.0.

JOWETT CARS LTD., IDLE, BRADFORD, YORKS.

The car was towed to the police station for examination. I was later summoned to attend court. The police officer read out a statement saying that the handbrake had been badly damaged over a period of time by the right-hand-side of the driver's seat, and, in doing so, prevented the brake being properly applied. The magistrate asked if I had anything to say, and in answering, I agreed that the seat was damaged but had no bearing on the brake operating.

A member of my company had attended the court in the public gallery. He shouted to the magistrate asking to be heard and, although most irregular, was granted permission to speak. He commented that the statement said that the brake was at the right-hand-side of the damaged driver's seat, but it was in the centre of the car. I was then asked to make an observation, to which I stated that the statement was correct and that the handbrake was on the right-hand-side. The case was dismissed but my friend in the gallery was fined £2 for contempt of court! Apart from the paintwork, there was very little damage to the car.

On having use of a company car in 1955, I regretfully had to sell my Jowett, which was acquired by two of my assistant engineers for the sum of £50. I wish I had kept it and how I wish Jowetts were still made!

Arthur Canfield, Bruton, Somerset

JR 5643

My first contact with a Jowett was in about 1930, through the headmaster of my first school. He had an early model, a long-four; I would have been eleven at the time. I was rather large for my age, and he would get me to 'wind her up'. There was no self-starter fitted in those days, so a starting handle had to be used. I was taught to keep my thumb over the handle in case it back-fired and would break it.

Our first Jowett was owned by my father and registered JR 5643, this was a 1937 '8'. The second was a 1939 '8' registered CN 8290. I ended up doing nearly 120,000 miles with JR 5643, much of which towing a heavy trailer.

My father used JR 5643 to tow a large trailer used in his wireless business. He would load the trailer with all his wireless gear for use on ships. This trailer was regularly hoisted into the air by crane straight into the hold of ships so the equipment was in the right place when he started work. He used this car right through the war; it was also used by me when I was on leave (I joined the TA in 1937 and was called up at the beginning of the war). My father, at the start of the war, realised that cars would be hard to find, so bought the 1939 model registered CN 8290 at a cost of £90. So during the war only one car was used at once, so both were kept in good condition. After the war he sold CN 8290 and bought a Vauxhall Velox, and I continued to use JR 5643.

We had a large caravan which we wanted to tow with the '8'; I remember my father was concerned that it would be too much for its twin-cylinder engine. So in early 1939 my father and I visited the Jowett factory in Idle, I was just twenty years old at the time. The first thing I saw on entering the factory was a large notice above our heads, which read 'We are at Idle but never Idle!' We were shown round the factory, like a pair of special guests, by one of the directors. He said it would be fine to fit a tow bar, as they were designed to go up hills, so the transmission could take the extra power required. He went on to say that if a hill was too steep for the car and caravan, we could always turn round and find another route, which of course we often did!

The only trouble we had was from over-heating, but when I fitted a fan it helped solve the problem. I also fitted two small blocks of wood to lift up the back of the bonnet to improve air circulation. On one trip we had a bit of a panic when the heat of the silencer set fire to the plywood floor and carpet under the passenger's seat. With a bit of quick thinking we put it out with a bottle of lemonade. From then on the inside of the car always smelt of lemons!

I have several amusing Jowett stories that come to mind, I hope you enjoy them also:-

1) In 1950 while living in Tyneside, we took two aged aunts on holiday around Scotland. There were four of us plus luggage. We drove to the Trossachs, up to Oban and Inverness and then started on our way back. We were at Balmoral when we heard a bang under the bonnet; we did not stop, but continued at a very slow pace. Going up hills, the passengers had to get out and walk, but we kept going on one cylinder. I took the plug lead off, which made no difference. We continued home very slowly, it was a bit difficult getting on and off the ferry over the Forth, next to the railway bridge. We eventually got home, travelling for about 150 miles on one cylinder. At home I took the head off to find the top of the piston had come off above the rings.

2) In 1952 JR 5643 had to make a number of journeys from Tyneside to Watford, as we were moving house. On one occasion on the Great North Road (no motorways in those days) we came to a halt. On lifting the bonnet I removed the distributor top and found that I could turn the shaft freely, as the drive had gone. I removed the assembly and found that the drive bevel gear was loose. It was held on by a split pin, which had broken. I walked to a nearby cottage with the wheel in my hand, found a suitable nail in a rusty old tin, and took it back to the car. I fitted it, bent it over and reassembled the lot. As the Jowett had an open flywheel with Top

Dead Centre marked, I retimed the engine at the same time. I was back on the road within fifteen minutes. It was over two years before I replaced this rusty nail!

3) A feature of the Jowett was that the front doors opened from from the back, and as there was no strap they would fold back against the rear door. In those days we all gave lifts to hitch-hikers. One night I gave a lift to a soldier. He was drunk, and became abusive when I would not take him miles out of my way. I slowed down near the curb, reached over and released his door catch. I gave him a good push and he was gone! I then touched the brake and the door swung back into place, then I was on my way again!

4) We were part of the Northern Jowett Car Club based in Newcastle between 1935 and 1939, we had seventeen members with '7's and '8's. We had regular rallies which included driving tests. We went to places like the Lake District, a distance of 100 miles each way. We also held picnics and competed for a trophy given to us by Jowett Cars Ltd. This was a large silver bowl about 12in across; it was supplied by Northern Goldsmiths of Newcastle. The yearly winners had the registration of their car engraved round the edge; we won it on three occasions so it became ours. It sat on our sideboard for many years, I just wish we had kept it!

5) My father used to visit a ship called *The Thomas Cook* on the Tyne; it was a small coaster that carried dynamite from Portmadoc in South Wales. Due to the danger, the coaster used to go up the Tyne, past all the houses of Newcastle, and unload in a remote field. There were no detonators, which was just as well, as all the men would smoke whilst unloading it. Their van was used to deliver the dynamite to the quarries and coal mines in the area. On one occasion

The Derby Winner.

The man who wins the Calcutta Sweep will be able to buy a Rolls. The man who doesn't, and there will be quite a few, will find that in the Jowett he has a car that doesn't need a plethoric bank balance behind it. . . . .

(The dots represent a squint at the dictionary to see what plethoric means.)

Efficiency and economy are what we aim at, with what success our Booklet "Owners' Opinions" (yours for a postcard) will tell you.

Our standard colours are maroon and royal blue, both very attractive, and the fitments, which are included in the price of the car, leave nothing to be desired.

The Jowett saloon is luxuriously upholstered, and rear blind, rope pulls, parcel net, etc., are standard. It is cool in summer and warm in winter, and you can drive a full day without a suggestion of stuffiness. Its price is £170.

Other models from £134.   Tax £7.

Dunlop Balloons and Stewart Speedometer Standard.

JOWETT CARS LTD., IDLE, BRADFORD.

my father was setting off for home down the long dirt track from the coaster to the main road. A gang of the men set off at the same time, so he gave them a lift, four men in the car with him and another nine in the trailer. This made a total of fourteen men, including my father, being driven in a Jowett at once – this must be some kind of record!

6) When I moved south to the Watford area, and to High Wycombe, which was my wife's home, we used to travel down on alternate weekends house hunting. I would teach all day on Friday, have a few hours sleep, then drive all night with the baby asleep in a carrycot on the back floor. The drive down would take nine hours, and on most occasions the baby would never wake up. We would then go house hunting on Saturday, then drive back on Sunday and back to school on Monday!

Sadly you find that these sorts of events are only memories, as I am now in my eighties, but I have had great pleasure in recalling them for you.

Leslie Beach, Croxley Green, Herts.

'Flossie'

I will have to start my story in 1938. My (future) husband at that time, was young, single and carefree and felt he was able to buy an almost new Ford 8. Of course, when the war started he was called up, (eventually he was to take part in the D-Day landings). The Ford was put on blocks in the garage to await happier times. When he was due for his first leave from Europe, I arranged for the local garage to get it ready for the road. In fact the man who sold him the car was happy to do the work needed, and to be part of the surprise! Forces coming on leave from Europe were allowed a few gallons of petrol. By that time we were married, and had a wonderful time pretending everything was normal!

A year after the hostilities, Stanley was demobbed, and arrived home with a derisory sum of money and a cheap suit. We decided that the Ford would have to go, to save money as, by then, the babies were arriving on the scene and we needed cots and prams etc. We did, however, miss having a car. In 1956 Stanley was offered a 1932 Jowett fabric-bodied saloon. The owner of the car said his wife would not go out in the car, so I do not know what that says about me! Anyway, Stanley bought it for £27.

When the car was taxed, insured and finally ours, we had to christen the car, so we called her 'Flossie'. She was not much to look at; we were not allowed to sit on the wheel arches so we would not damage the fabric body. She did, however, take Stanley to work, twelve miles return, each day. She also served as an alarm call for the neighbours, as she did not glide silently away, but made a lot of fuss about getting started and onto the road! Once going though, she gave us no trouble.

She took seven of us (that included my mum and dad) to Rhyl or Prestatyn most Sundays that summer. She did, however, need a bit of regular maintenance and our son, then aged seven, helped and soon knew all Flossie's inner parts. This must have given him his life-long interest in car engines, though he has a new car at the moment.

We went for many sight-seeing trips, apart from the seaside, including trips to Wiltshire and to Manchester on many occasions. I remember one evening we were waiting at a junction and a bus pulled up beside us. Stanley said, 'that driver cannot believe his eyes, as I have more passengers than he has!'

It was a sad time when we had to part with Flossie, but it became more difficult improvising her bits and pieces, and she became no longer viable. These were happy days and I have enjoyed remembering them for you.

Mrs Brenda Clarke, Alsager, Stoke-on-Trent

'Clara Clutterbuck'

My father had two Jowetts: a Javelin and long-four. The earlier model was affectionately known as 'Clara Clutterbuck', though as an eleven-year-old I can remember asking my parents to park round the corner if they came to collect me from school. I just wanted nobody I knew seeing me getting into such an ancient vehicle! I am sure my reaction would be very much different now.

I'm afraid I cannot give you any technical details apart from the fact that Clara dated from 1926. I remember groups of enthusiasts gathering around her and peering lovingly into the engine, quite a mystery to me at the time, though I too appreciate older things much more now!

Annette Taylor, Colchester

HFH 316

I acquired my second car in 1933; it was a 1923 Jowett short-two with room in the front for three and two in the dickey seat behind. It had a canvas hood and celluloid side-screens. This was similar in design to my first car – a 1914 Wolseley, which I had bought in 1927 – that is to say three in the front and two in the dickey. As mentioned, the Jowett was ten years old when I bought it, but I enjoyed driving it for two years. I swapped this in 1935 for a 1933 Austin Seven; I did not like this car as it was so cramped compared to the Jowett. I only had this car for eighteen months before changing it for a 1935 Jowett Black Prince, which I paid £120 for.

I was happy again as the car had my great friend, the twin-cylinder 7hp horizontally-opposed engine, fitted. It also had a full four-seater saloon body and sliding roof. When fully-laden, I am sure it could have driven up the side of my house if the wheels would have held! The huge springs in the rear seat were a great joy to the children, who loved to bounce up and down on them, but never caused any damage. The car was later stored for three years during the war.

The 1926 long-four known as Clara Clutterbuck *owned by the late Dr Geoffrey Poole, taken outside the family home, beside his new Javelin.*

My brother, having founded the firm Page & Davies, became the main Jowett agents in Gloucester, and soon after the war he put my name down for the new Javelin, which had been announced to the public, but was still not available.

In 1947, on leaving the RAF, I applied for a five-year post as a science lecturer at an Emergency Teacher Training College opening in North Staffordshire. I was given the job, accordingly let my property in Gloucester, and moved my wife and two small daughters to college accommodation. 360 students arrived for the thirteen-month course; they were all ex-servicemen, all most anxious to be returned to civilian life, so there was no need to stimulate their thirst for knowledge! I lectured and organised practical laboratory work and initiated societies such as rocks & fossils, aquarist, beekeeping, cacti growing and tried to cater for other interests in science aspects.

The teacher training gave us our own experiences in schools, placing and visiting the students during their three to five week placements in Birmingham, Wolverhampton and Stoke-on-Trent. This meant miles of travel for me in my 1935 twin-cylinder Black Prince.

Towards the end of the course of the second intake of students, our thirty-three staff were told that we had run out of raw material, as most ex-servicemen had by then found it impossible to wait any longer for the course and so found work elsewhere. You can imagine the panic of those of us that had sold their houses and moved to the area. We managed to keep going into 1949, but were saved as new courses were set up for girls. The first intake was on 1 October 1949, which was for 150 eighteen-year-old girls on two and three-year courses.

Soon after this I took delivery of my new Javelin; it was registered HFH 316, it was a wonderful car, which I appreciated even more than the Black Prince. I used the car for many years and found it was ideal for towing a caravan. I used it to take the caravan on touring holidays in England, Scotland and Wales. I ran the car for fifteen years, but in 1964 it developed a fault and became harder and harder to start. I sold the car to a local coach driver, who took the engine out and stripped it. He later came round to see me to show me what the problem was. The manifold had worn so thin with wear that it was allowing air into the mixture. It was a simple repair for him and he continued to use the car for weekend trips to Wales, boasting continually how he kept beating his own record time for the 200-mile trip! He carried on like this for two years until the engine was worn out, and beyond economic repair.

My car love had then to be transferred, as by 1964, Jowett had long gone, and the Maxi became my favourite car I owned since the Jowetts. I am now running an Accord, but it lacks that assured contentment of my dear old Javelin.

The first group of girls to come to the college formed a club called 'The Forty Niners', and last October the club held a reunion. They are all aged seventy-ish now, but sixty-eight of them turned up for the weekend at a hotel in Oxford. My wife and I were guests of honour. They all remembered how I turned up at the college with the Javelin. I was presented with a framed picture of a red Javelin and a birthday cake in the form of a beehive, as many of them had joined my apiary club and gone on to be beekeepers for many years. I had never been kissed so much in all my life and could only say I wished they had started sooner! – I am now ninety-three years old.

Roy Page, Weymouth, Dorset

BOB 669

My father, Charles Marvin, was born in 1913 in Brierley Hill, Staffs and started driving when he was nineteen years old in 1932. He never took a driving test, as his licence pre-dated the requirement to do so. He stopped driving in 1982 when he moved to York. He owned two Jowetts in the 1930s, the first being a *c.*1926 long-four registered UN 4055, the second was a *c.*1935 Kestrel registered BOB 669.

He has asked me to pass on these three anecdotes, which he hopes are accurate:

1) In the summer of 1935, whilst my mother was getting ready to go shopping, he adjusted the clutch on the long-four by loosening the clutch assembly, threading asbestos cord through and tightening it up again.

2) When returning from holiday in July 1934, approaching Bristol, I thought everybody was being very friendly, waving to us; there was in fact smoke coming from the brakes!

The 1936 long-bodied saloon of Charles Marvin, registered BOB 669, pictured in the Ellam Valley in 1939.

Another view of BOB 669.

3) In August 1934 I set off with my friend, Gilbert Shuttleworth, for Brooklands to see some motorcycle racing, a rare event at the time. When approaching Oxford, the engine suffered a major breakdown. We had to leave the car at a local garage and come home by train. The following week we towed the car home with the help of the next-door neighbour, who also obtained the spares and helped us rebuild the engine.

Andrew Marvin, York

'Joey Jowett'

My father bought our Jowett car in the 1920s; we were living in Bolton at the time. We travelled thousands [of miles] all over the country on touring holidays every Sunday between April and October. We met up with four or five other families, [their cars] all more high powered than ours but the Jowett was the only one never to need running repairs, except for punctures, while on the road. Its petrol consumption was so small our friends used to say, 'I think Joey Jowett runs on cold tar'.

The car had a maroon leatherette body with metal bonnet and wings. A starting handle was kept under the front bench seat; there was no door on the driver's side. There was a windscreen wiper, which you had to move by hand. If it rained very hard, snowed or in fog you had to open the top half of the screen. In real pea-soupers one of us had to walk in front of the car.

I think we went over every pass in the Lake District, Yorkshire Dales, Derbyshire and Wales and the only time I remember dad have the family get out and walk was on a loose surface road, travelling up to Malham bore. Our friends stood at the top and cheered as Dad drove up!

I learned to drive in this car and mastered the art of the double-declutch to change gears, going up and down hills. Also giving hand signals, as there were no trafficators fit-

The long-four of Mr Tom Downing, taken in 1928, while on a tour up the Wye Valley to Mid and North Wales. The picture shows Mrs Downing and her daughter, Joyce. It was Joyce who sent the picture in.

ted. The roads in those days did not have white lines or cats eyes, and many with deep ditches running down each side. I am still driving after seventy years, but avoid cities now.

I have owned many makes of car over the years but I think the Jowett days were the best, or should I say, most exciting. Having said that, I would not like to go back to cranking the car up by hand, opening the windscreen in bad weather, mending inner tubes and pumping up tyres. I often wonder how we did it!

Miss Eileen Cooper, Lytham St Annes

A long-four and a Kestrel

My father, Tom Downing, started driving in the 1920s and always sang the praises of the Jowett cars he owned before the war, the first car being a Jowett long-four. In 1928 my mother and father toured from Hertfordshire, through the West Country, and up the Wye Valley to Mid and North Wales for our summer holiday. Those were the days when villages in the West Country, let alone Wales, seemed absolutely remote, and, when you met AA patrolmen on their motorbikes and sidecars, they saluted every member.

The later car was a Kestrel registered BGK 629, and it took four adults and a twelve-year-old plus luggage on a trip to Wales in 1935.

My father used to do his own repairs in the early days and would disappear for hours to the garage. He had to rent the garage, as none of the houses had garages then. This garage was one of eight at the edge of some woodland some distance from the houses. It was safe to leave a car from one week to the next and you did not hear of break-ins or damage. How times have changed!

Joyce Illett, Bexley, Kent

The Kestrel of Tom Downing, registered BGK 629, on a steep pass called Bwlch-Y-Groes on 13 August 1935.

The Kestrel taken at the same time from the rear. The people at the back of the car are Joyce's grandparents.

A fleet of twenty-seven long-fours were sold to the Metropolitan Police in 1926. The cars were driven down in convoy, stopping at local Jowett agents on the way down, to obtain maximum publicity! This picture was taken outside Ewins Motor Agents, Banbury.

Police Jowetts

Early one morning in the early 1930s I was standing on the pavement in Whetstone High Road in North London; this was a wide thoroughfare. In the centre of the road there was a Jowett long-four police car with two burley policemen inside with their right arms outstretched, waiting to turn right into a side road.

I saw a motor coach travelling at about 40mph in a direct line for the rear of the Jowett. There was ample room to pass on the nearside, but to my amazement it rammed into the back of the Jowett. The strength of the impact pushed the car 15yds past the side road. The two bobbies staggered out of the car, with their helmets still in place!

The coach driver was from Blackpool and had virtually had no rest in the previous forty-eight hours. He was charged with dangerous driving at Highgate Court and was sacked.

Reg Reeve, Shaftsbury, Dorset

[*In 1926 Jowetts supplied twenty-seven long-fours to the Metropolitan Police. One of these still survives, and this account would appear to confirm how one of them met their demise! NS*]

AK 9417

I am eighty-two years old, born and bred in Bradford! My father, Jack Cartright, was one of the first 100 workers at Jowett Cars Ltd. He was the foreman of the cutting department in the upholstery shop. He spent many hours designing the door panels, roof and seats. He also went to the Motor Show most years. My uncle, Johnny Williams, was also a foreman joiner and my two cousins also worked there in the office.

In 1927 my father bought a two-seater Jowett car with dickey seat. This is where I sat if weather permitted, otherwise I sat on a small stool between my parents, with strict instructions not to touch! My mother was a no-speed freak; when the speedometer reached 30mph she would loudly point this out to my dad!

Our outings were to Morecombe, which was an early start on a Sunday morning. On other occasions, dad would pick me up from Sunday school and we would go to Ilkley or Otley. My mother would have some peace at home! I particularly enjoyed the Sundays when it was raining; I can still recall the smell of the leather, it seemed stronger when it rained!

My father and my uncle caused quite a stir in the neighbourhood when they set off for Wales, just before Christmas. I think it took them two days; the rest of the family travelled by train. I know we were all relieved when they made it home again after Christmas.

The car was sold in 1928; the coming slump was evident to my father. I think the car's registration number was AK 9417, but I could have confused things over the years. We continued to live in Bradford, but moved to Five Lane Ends in Idle, the home of Jowett Cars Ltd. My father stayed on with Jowetts after the war, and later with International Harvester when they took over in 1954.

I realise this is more of a chronicle of the Jowett company, rather than of my experience of the car, but Jowetts played a major part in my life, as I grew up.

Mrs Hilda Cochrane (née Cartright), Preston, Lancashire

DUA 442

I was demoted from the Royal Army Medical Corps during the summer of 1949 and by the following year I was impatient to have my own 'wheels'.

The first car I bought was a 1935 7hp Jowett; it was in dire straits with neither rear mudguards, headlamps, nor starter motor – and the engine was tired!

Fitting new cylinders and pistons, making a pair of rear wings and fitting them together, and with one very large spot lamp plus painting the whole car, all of this put the old Jowett back on the road. Starting was by use of the handle; it needed a new starter and flywheel gear and I never got round to doing that before I was offered a substantial profit on what I had paid for it – so it had to go. The profit was burning a hole in my pocket and it was fortunate that DUA 442 was taken in part exchange at Jack Briggs & Son of Castleford, where my father was a car salesman. The deal was struck and the car was mine for the princely sum of £125.

DUA 442 was a black 1936 saloon with a 7hp s.v. flat-twin of 17bhp at 2,800rpm, with a spare wheel in the 'boot' which had a drop-down lid for luggage, a sliding roof, opening windscreen, twin wipers and chromed bumpers – I believe it was a de luxe model. It was in very reasonable condition considering that it was already fifteen or so years old; its only fault when I took delivery was that the speedometer didn't work although, at 45,000 miles, the mileometer did. This unit was removed, and with a reconditioned Smiths obtained from Owen Owens of Pontefract, my motoring with DUA started at zero miles! When I finally sold it in 1959, the Jowett had been round the clock and stood at over 20,000; its 120,000+ miles in my hands had never seen a breakdown to the extent of having to be recovered or towed in (it once tried but didn't succeed – that's a story for later...).

51

Ken Bramald's 1935 7hp Jowett.

I started to use DUA for commuting to my place of work at the Public Health Laboratory in Wakefield in the building of the W. Riding County Medical Officers Dept., where it joined just three other cars in the car park. It was also used as a band-wagon; at that time I was playing the drums in a small jazz band at dance gigs around the area, so it carried my drum kit, tenor and alto saxophones, and usually the pianist and band library. The other players made their way to the venue by public transport and shared a taxi home afterwards. Summer Sundays usually saw up to four of the band on days out to the Yorkshire coast: Scarborough, Filey, Bridlington or one of the many beaches in that area. And it was on a return journey from one such outing that I was involved in my first (and, to this day, only) accident.

It had been a particularly busy Sunday in Bridlington and I had anticipated crowded roads on the journey home so, making use of my map, I opted to take a minor road for the first part of the journey, leaving the Bridlington-Filey A165 to go across country to Kirkham and then on to the A64 for York. Whether this route would have given me the quiet road home that I sought I shall never know; certainly the first part was traffic-free – that is until I reached an unmarked crossroads at Butterwick! Before I knew what was happening a Morris 8 was bearing down on my nearside and with an almighty crash the Jowett was turning onto its side and sliding across the road to a standstill. In that short time the driver's door had opened and, with my nearside passenger falling on top of me and half-pushing me out of my open door, the car fell onto that door thus closing it with my right arm still outside. My three passengers were unhurt but I sustained a simple fracture to my right arm radius bone and that required a trip in an ambulance to Driffield Hospital and an overnight stay.

DUA 442 was a write-off and the police

had it removed to the local garage at Weaverthorpe. My father called to see it after he had been to see me in hospital, and arranged with the garage owner for it to be made safe for towing back home to Wakefield. Later he and a colleague did a rigid tow with his Jowett 8 and DUA was back in its garage with the door quietly closed. I was absolved of any misdemeanour since the Morris driver had ignored a 'Slow X-Roads Ahead' sign and my approach to the crossroads was unmarked. The insurance company paid me out and allowed me to keep the wreck; six weeks later and with my arm repaired and my cycle overhauled I was mobile again, and thoughts turned to what to do with DUA.

Repairing it to its original condition was out of the question, so the first job was to establish how much serious structural damage had been done. I started to dismantle the bodywork in the following order: doors and boot lid, windscreen, rear and then front mudguards, bonnet and radiator, all seats and floorboards, sliding roof, then removed all of the body to the chassis bolts and cut through the tops of both screen and centre door pillars and through the roof sides above the rear door openings.

The parts were then in a manageable size to take off the chassis and store away, and with the chassis stripped the damage was now obvious; very bent where it had taken the full force of the Morris 8! What to do next? The local Ford dealers were the agent for, I think, Rubery Owen, a chassis maker and repairer who assured me that they could undertake to restore DUA's chassis to as new as specification and alignment. So I could, with a little work and at reasonable expense, finish up with a rolling chassis in good order. But could I then build a body for this chassis that I would be prepared to ride in?

I have always enjoyed a challenge, and endowed with some skills in wood and metalwork, I decided to give it my best effort.

The original DUA 422.

The engine, gearbox, back and front axles, steering gear, and all other bits were stripped off and the chassis sent for reconditioning. While it was away I checked and cleaned all the mechanical parts, repairing and replenishing as and when necessary, and in my quieter moments planned the new body.

It was obvious that the body had to be as simple as possible from the construction point of view, and also the lighter the better for the size and the power of the engine. A shooting brake body was therefore out and the stance of the chassis prevented the adoption of a very sporting two-seater with cycle-type wings. The answer was a two-door four-seater soft top coupe with a smaller area than the old saloon but with a bigger boot to fill up the length of the chassis. The first thing to do was to repair the nearside front wing, which had suffered badly in the crash. I then started building in new scuttle-pillars to create a new windscreen frame to carry the existing but re-glazed opening windscreen, this was then fixed to the new chassis side and floor frame boards and the old scuttle fastened to the new windscreen frame. At this point the radiator, bonnet and the dashboard were fitted so that the steering box, column and the wheel could be replaced. I now had the makings of a rolling chassis. The body frame measurements to the rear of the door opening were now established and construction in ash and elm was slowly put in-hand. I could add at this point that all of this work was taking place in a small wooden building with an earthen floor. The property to which it was attached – my parents' house – did not have any power other than gas. So all of my cutting, drilling, sawing and sanding of both wood and metal was done by hand and the only light that I had to work with was a Tilly paraffin lamp. New floorboards were made from plywood, a metal rear seat pan fitted, new inner-ear wheel

covers fabricated and fitted, together with a new floor for the boot (the spare wheel was to be carried on the outside of the boot). New door frames were made and hung on large domestic brass hinges, but the locks and all handles were transferred from the old body.

It was now time to think about panelling the frame and sufficient 22-gauge aluminium for the purpose was purchased, with strips of thin felt glued to the contact area of the frame to prevent it rattling. The sheets of aluminium were cut to size to allow a turnover which was pinned to the wood with brass shoe-nails; a boot lid frame was made and covered in aluminium and it too was fitted with domestic hinges and closed by 'cabin trunk over centre' catches complete with locks. It was now starting to look like a car but there was still a lot to do. The front and rear wings and a new pair of running boards covered in rubber mat with new finishing mouldings were fitted, together with headlamps and sidelamps with new wiring loom. All new inner panelling was made from three-ply covered in thin felt and dark green leather cloth and held in place with upholstery cup washers and dome-head chromed screws. The new windscreen frame was covered with trim made from aluminium covered with leather cloth and secured with washers and screws. With all the seats fitted I was now able to spark it up and run it up and down the private lane to our house, a matter of some 50yds. It was a runner and only needed finishing off, so the bumpers were fitted with the number plates, rear lamps, trafficators and rear view mirrors.

The design of the hood frame had occupied my thoughts for some time but the problem was finally solved by the use of a sliding support for the upright frame that abutted the rear of the side windows; this device allowed the frame hoops to fold back on top of each other behind the rear seat

DUA 442 after its accident.

squab. The making of the hood was contracted out to a local upholstery and hood specialist from Cheapside in Wakefield. He came out to see the task, went back to his workshop, then returned a week later and fitted the hood. It was a most beautiful job. There were just two things left to do, sidescreens for the doors, and a new paint job. The sidescreens were a temporary lash-up, simple non-opening wooden frames covered in celluloid sheet, to be later replaced by something more convenient. The car was painted with Dulux coach enamel in British Racing Green over black wings. Taxed and insured, I was back on the road, and it had taken me something in the order of 600 hours of labour. I did get one thing radically wrong in the design, I took the level for the top of the doors from the centre of the windscreen bottom frame and this, of course, was carried through to the rear of the body but the finished result was a couple of inches too high. When I stood back and looked at it, it was all too obvious

but too late to alter so that was how it stayed. Other than that it all worked very well and presented no problems; it didn't rattle or leak rainwater, and was draughtproof but it was cold in winter, like so many other cars of that era, until I fitted a heater of limited output which did make long winter journeys more comfortable.

Refurbished, DUA 442 commuted me to work, to professional studies, and on recreational journeys at weekends and holidays which were all unremarkable until my father and I bought a small caravan. It was one of the first that Willerby had made after the war and it was named the 'York'. Its construction (mostly from ex-War Ministry materials) suggested that it might be light in weight since it had a tubular steel frame and chassis, covered with doped and painted canvas with perspex windows. It was a small two-berth model and rode on low-pressure tyres on aircraft aluminium wheels.

I had a towing bracket constructed and fitted in readiness for towing, but instead of

The 1935 Jowett registered DUA 442, as re-bodied by Ken Bramald into a four-seater Tourer. It was painted in green with black mudguards. This picture was taken in Snowdonia. Ken's wife is on the right and her sister on the left. The flag on the front reads 'We've Been Everywhere!'

straight extensions from the Jowett chassis (which would have meant cutting holes in the new bodywork), I designed it to be cranked so as to pass under the boot and up to the bumper. On the first test run DUA towed the York quite well until the bracket broke at one of the welded cranks! Back to the drawing board, and straight extensions and holes through the body produced a much stronger tow bar. This experience suggested that the caravan could be lighter and I replaced all the furniture panelling, which was chipboard, with thin three-ply wood.

A colleague from work and I set off with this unlikely outfit for a holiday in Cornwall, but when we got as far as Coventry a caravan wheel collapsed. Scouring the scrap yards found us an 'easyclean' wheel from a Morris 8, complete with tyre which would fit.

Continuing on our way in the Jowett, and two punctures later, we revised our destination plans and came to rest in Paignton in Devon. We enjoyed two weeks there and returned via the Cotswolds where the Jowett and caravan had to be helped by a Land Rover up two of the hills on the Foss Way. This was a sharp lesson in power-to-weight ratios; the York was sold on returning home, complete with its odd wheels.

During the winter of 1954/55 two colleagues and myself attended vocational education evening classes in Sheffield, a round trip of fifty miles twice a week, and DUA was pressed into service again, thus clocking up the best part of 5,000 miles for the sake of knowledge! These were the days when, on leaving Sheffield after the classes, we would pull up into the first available lay-by, pour out the coffee from the flasks, tune in my portable radio and listen to the Goon Show. The remainder of the journey would be spent not on remembering the lessons of the class, but the humour of the Goons.

In 1956, at the time of the Suez Crisis and the return of petrol rationing, I was courting a young lady (later to be my wife) who lived in Huddersfield. I still lived in Lofthouse near Wakefield, so a round trip to see my girlfriend of about thirty miles was made two or three times a week, so soon had the petrol ration finished. Necessity being the mother of invention, I soon had the problem solved. I converted DUA to run on Calor gas, and it was really so simple and worked first time with little modification that I was astounded. First I fitted a motorcycle petrol on/off tap in the pipe from the petrol pump to the carburettor, this was fitted with a stiff wire extension from the tap which went into the car near the dashboard so that it could be opened from inside. Next a half-inch domestic gas tap was mounted,

again near the dashboard, which was to be the main control. This was connected by a half-inch gas pipe to a 32lb Calor gas cylinder in the boot of the car using a normal caravan regulator. A similar half-inch gas tap was mounted on the inside of the offside wing valance in line with the carburettor, and its handle had an extension strip of metal fastened to it with a series of holes in its length. A connection to the accelerator rod was made and hinged to one of the holes in the extension strip, so the accelerator operated the gas tap in the same ratio as the throttle (the ratio could be adjusted by using other holes in the gas tap operating extension strip). I picked the right one first time! The cylinder to the main on/off tap, then to accelerator tap, and finally to the air intake on the carburettor, was by half-inch rubber pipe. Switch on, start up on petrol, switch off the petrol, and when the engine faltered, turn on the gas – it ran perfectly! A road test showed a little less performance and an unreliable tick-over, but the latter was cured

The rear view of Ken Bramald's re-bodied 1935 Jowett. I think he made an excellent job of it, what a shame it is no longer with us.

Repenting at leisure

is not indulged in by Jowett owners. Alone (we believe) amongst manufacturers we publish a folder which gives the intending purchaser full details of his expenses in running one of our cars. This should be studied by all who are dubious as to their financial ability to run a car. It is a very pleasant thing to us to receive, very frequently, letters from Jowett owners stating they are running their cars at a cheaper rate than is shown by our folder.

We say, very definitely, that it is impossible to motor more cheaply than on a Jowett.

There is no light car more reliable. Or so efficient.

For twenty-one years we have fought for economical motoring, and in buying a Jowett you buy this experience.

Decide on a Jowett now. You will never repent.

Short two, £134.　　　　Long two, £142.
Chummy, £142.　　　　Full four, £145.
Sports, £145.　Coupé, £168.　Saloon, £170.

Dunlop Balloons and Stewart Speedometers standard.

May we send our interesting literature ?

JOWETT CARS LTD., IDLE, BRADFORD

by fitting a thin rubber pipe to bypass the accelerator-operated gas tap, which had a pinch-screw clamp that could be adjusted to give more reliable slow running. A further modification was to fit another 32lb cylinder in tandem, both feeding through caravan regulators into a gallon oil can then into the main feedpipe.

Unfortunately, the petrol crisis was during the winter months, and at the prevailing low temperatures on a long journey the rapid removal of gas from the cylinders lowered its temperature still more until the gas froze (propane was not readily available then or this would not have been a problem). But the fifteen miles to Huddersfield was possible, and after a rest period for the cylinders to thaw out, so was the return home. It was on one such journey home, on this occasion using a drop of my petrol ration, that DUA tried to break down and leave me stranded. Seconds before the engine died I heard a funny metallic sound. Opening the bonnet showed nothing amiss, plenty of ignition spark, so it must be petrol starvation. I worked the hand primer on the pump which filled the carburettor, started up, and drove a few yards, only for it to stop again! So I switched on the gas, started up once more, and drove home. The following day I took off the petrol pump to find that the metal finger, which engaged with the camshaft, had broken at the pivot hole and was somewhere in the sump (funny metallic sound!). I was able to obtain a new finger for the pump, which I refitted, so I was soon back on the road. My earlier comments that DUA had 'tried to break down and failed' are now explained. The gas conversion was removed at the end of petrol rationing.

Continuous reliable service I had come to expect from DUA, the only normal replacement of parts that became worn were part of its upkeep. I remember fitting new king-pins and bushes, and new rear shock absorbers of the Luvax type but filled not with oil but some sort of uncured rubber (they were very stiff for quite a long time). I replaced the odd broken leaf spring, did regular de-cokes and replaced the occasional exhaust valve, but I needed a continuous supply of springs for the engine mountings. Cobbled up repairs kept the exhaust system serviceable and gas tight.

On one holiday in Cornwall we had been touring in the Lands End area, and we were approaching St Buryan when I thought we were being buzzed by a light aircraft, but I soon realised that the din was coming from DUA. Examination showed that one of the exhaust pipes had broken through about 3in from the cylinder. Gently driving the last few yards into the village, we found a roadside blacksmith who agreed to do a weld if I removed the pipe. Half an hour later and half a crown lighter we were back on the road to Penzance. The whole time I owned and ran the Jowett it never required any attention to the main bearings or big ends, the clutch, gearbox or back axle. The tyres were replaced one at a time when absolutely necessary and always by remoulds, and the brakes were realigned by the Close Asbestos Co. (and latterly included a strip of packing between the shoes and the linings to take up the wear in the drums!).

In March 1958 I took my wife and I on honeymoon to London and on our return home to Flockton it had a longer journey to take me to work. At about this time I noticed an increase in oil consumption and decided that it was time for a re-bore and new pistons; Parkinson's, 'The Rider Dealers' (Motorcycles) in Wakefield undertook to do the work at the cost of 30 shillings per cylinder including the new pistons and rings. So I took the cylinders off the engine and took them in two carrier bags on the bus to Parkinson's, and after work on the same day collected them ready to replace. Running-in on the first day back to work, I found the car going slower and slower until, with a loud squeaking, the engine seized. I waited a few minutes for the engine to cool then I restarted it. Having stopped close to a filling station I purchased a pint of two-stroke self-mixing oil, poured this into the petrol tank, gave the car a good shake, and continued my journey to work. All was alright so obviously the new scraper rings had been doing their job too well, and for the next 500 miles I added a little engine oil to the petrol and had no more trouble.

I did ask DUA to tow again but this time it was a very lightweight folding caravan, a two-berth Wessex borrowed from an acquaintance. The Jowett took it to Abersoch in North Wales without any trouble save for boiling on a long hill on the return trip in Snowdonia between Beddgelert and Betwys-y-Coed. DUA was starting to feel its age by now, amidst the Morris Minors, Austin A30s, Standard 8s, Ford Anglias, Prefects and similar cars of the day. I had on occasion driven all of these and

MG TD's and Triumph TR2s and the performance of the small affordable cars was quite remarkable. The opportunity to purchase a 1956 Austin A30 Countryman was taken, and the Jowett was offered for sale. A gentleman who said he was a religious missionary working in Africa, but home on leave for a few months, was wanting a cheap reliable car for that time, he became the new owner for £45. I never saw DUA 442 again.

Ken Bramald, Wakefield

A keen supporter

My father was a very keen supporter of Jowett cars. He was a Yorkshireman – a Congregational Minister – and we lived in Scarborough from 1922-1928. He had very little money so his car had to be economical. He bought his first Jowett 7 in about 1923 or 1924. In his view the most economical way to run his car was to trade it in every two or three years for a new one, and I well remember having at least two blue Jowetts while we lived in Scarborough.

`The Horrox family in their long-four, registered KU 1471, taken in the summer of 1926 on the road to Buttermere.*

The Horrox family taken in 1927 or 1928, in their long-four, registered YR 2413, on the Cockhill Moors near Haworth.

Mr and Mrs Horrox in their c.1929 long-four, registered GC 5447, in about July 1930.

Another view of GC 5447.

Unfortunately the first registration number of which I have a record is KU 1417. He certainly had that car in 1926 when we had a family holiday in the Lake District. The photograph of that car shows the road on the way to Buttermere. His cars were driven over many moorland roads and hills, and I know he was always delighted at how well they performed. In 1928 we moved to Portsmouth and he later bought his next Jowett which was a tan car, registration number GC 5447.

In about 1932 he was persuaded to try a small Rover – this was when saloons were just appearing. He had more trouble with that car than with all the others put together and he traded it in about a year for another Jowett 7. This was the first Jowett saloon he had had and the registration number was, I think, RV 7312 (but I am only relying on memory). That car also served him well and in 1936 we moved to Stockport.

In about 1936 or 1937 he traded in that car and got another Jowett, a black saloon ENB 607. Because of the war he could not follow his usual routine and exchange the cars every two or three years, and he ran the black saloon until it needed quite a bit spending on it. He sold it privately to someone in the Manchester area, but I do not know to whom. As all of these other Jowetts had been traded in to a garage, I have no idea of their eventual fate.

After the war Jowetts had stopped making the Jowett 7, and the Jupiter and Javelin were way above my father's pocket. Eventually he picked up a little 1932 two-seater Morris Minor second-hand. He was very disappointed at not being able to continue with Jowetts. My father looked after his cars very well and although I had been driving during the war years, I was not allowed to touch his cars. There was one emergency when he was arriving back in Manchester too late to catch the last train home and I was asked to drive his car into Manchester to pick him up. That was the only occasion on which I drove a Jowett car. I certainly have very happy memories of enjoyable outings in the Jowett cars and, on our yearly visits to Yorkshire from Portsmouth, my father usually called into the Jowett works at Idle.

Miss Elsie M. Horrox, Marlow, Bucks

CDE 191

When I lived in Wales in the 1950s my father, John Henry Daniels, owned a 1937 Jowett, CDE 191. I bought it from him in 1956 for £100. (I was earning £70 a month at the time, so it was a lot of money.) As the Suez Crisis had occurred around that time, I was able to drive with learner plates unaccompanied, as it was difficult to have a driving test. The car had a two-cylinder, horizontally-opposed engine, and went like a bomb. She was dark green originally, but had a paint job, which was a much lighter green, somewhat like the colour of the Lyles Golden Syrup can! She had four doors, and the indicator arms regularly went wrong, and often only half retracted. The seats were leather, and the passenger side one had problems, which were solved with a brick to support it.

I had numerous adventures with her (she was called 'Edna', after a friend of my father's). At one time on a trip from London to Pembrokeshire, the rear tyre burst and the spare wasn't in very good condition. I had to buy a new tyre, which unfortunately was slightly larger than its correct size. It played havoc with the speedometer and eventually I was able to buy the proper tyre and keep the other as a spare.

The car was regularly serviced at a small garage in Walkern, Hertfordshire. The owner was very familiar with Jowetts, and was able to keep her running. The worst thing that happened was when the crankshaft broke, and went right through the housing. My father contributed to the repairs, as it was put down to 'metal fatigue'. I lived in Stevenage on Hydean Way at the time I owned the car, and I used to park on an area of wasteland that had not been built on just behind the house. It was quite near a bus stop, and often in the morning, having sat outside all night, the car wouldn't start. I had to crank it, which was not an easy job, and sometimes it had to be pushed to get it started. I used to ask the people at the bus stop to help, which they usually did, but I noticed some of them chose a bus stop farther away!

In December 1959, for my swan song, just before I left for a teaching job in Hong Kong, I drove to a local school in Stevenage and unfortunately parked too close to a plate glass window near the front door and cracked it. My insurance company paid for that, my one and only accident in the UK. As I was leaving the country in January 1960, I needed to sell Edna and was offered £50 for her. The young man who bought her kept her for a few years but I fear she went to the scrap yard eventually

Owning a Jowett as my first car was a wonderful experience, as I had to learn to double-declutch and really got to know how the engine worked. Once there was a hole in the manifold, which had to be temporarily plugged with a thick toothpick to enable me to drive to the garage. The most dangerous thing I ever did was when there was a problem with the carburettor, and we couldn't get the gas to go through, so a garage rigged up a little gas tank with a piece of rubber pipe attached to the carburettor, and I had to keep stopping to unkink the pipe so we could drive the next few miles. How it didn't set on fire I will never know!

Miss Brenda Daniels, Oakville,
Ontario, Canada

Jowett's 4-light
BRADFORD
van or utility

A roomy well-lit 93 cu. ft. capacity van—tenacious reliability and the slogging power of the famous horizontally opposed twin cylinder engine make it ready for hard work in any climate. The 4-light body has sliding side windows. When supplied as a 6-seater utility the cost per person per mile bears comparison with any other form of transport, thanks to the Bradford's remarkable petrol economy.
Colours : Green, Blue or Grey with Black Wings.

stands up sturdily
to conditions anywhere in the world

2 The Bradford
The willing workhorse

A Bradford milk van

After my demob I started work on a dairy farm in Meshaw, North Devon, where we started milk delivery. Trying to find suitable small vans at that time was difficult. My father was born and bred in Queensbury near Bradford, and had a 'contact' at Jowett Cars in Idle, Bradford. So it was, a little later, that a new Bradford van was delivered by Jowetts to North Devon!

It was the ideal vehicle for the stop-start application of a milk round, and was still going strong when I emigrated to Northern Rhodesia in 1951.

Nothing to do with cars, but my maternal grandfather, who farmed at Ploughcraft Farm, Boothtown (near Halifax), was Albert Jowett – there may be a connection somewhere!

Bill Dobson, Kwazulu, Natal, South Africa

MPK 351

In 1958 I went on holiday with my parents in their Jowett Bradford van, which was registered MPK 351, to Hayling Island. I was eleven years old at the time.

Subsequently, the family ventured further afield to holidays in Cornwall, when the journey from Whitton (Twickenham) to Par (Cornwall) was made overnight.

After many hours of motoring, when my father's overtaking became reckless (probably passing a tractor) and my mother's nerves frayed, he would finally agree to stop for a rest, but only after the 'target' lay-by had been reached! (It's still there actually.)

For this epic journey my father constructed a 'stretcher'-type bed across the van between the back seat and the front seat. My small brother slept on the stretcher and I 'slept' on the back seat.

For us this was a real adventure, but the real excitement really started when, in the early light of morning, we arrived at the top of Penpillick Hill to see St Austell Bay laid out in front of us – we had arrived! As a Londoner, little did I ever believe that I was destined to live in Cornwall – my husband and I have been here for thirty-two years!

Sue Cox, Saltash, Cornwall

KPF 926

In the mid-1950s I purchased a Bradford van registered KPF 926 or 963, with windows in the side and fitted with bench seats in the back [*this was the Utility model, NS*]. It was used extensively for taking the children to school and collecting half a ton of chicken food once a month.

I was also given by a local farmer in Surrey, where we were living at the time, the wreck of another Bradford van out of one of his fields. The engine was still in good condition and ran well. This engine finally found its way into my original van, after I had blown the other one up after a high-speed chase to catch a train!

I eventually sold the original Bradford for scrap, but I used the chassis of the one pulled out of a field as a four-wheeled trailer on my small holding here. It's still going strong today!

David G. Forsyth, Launceston, Cornwall

PRE 905

The Bradford I drove whilst working for our firm, which was an offshoot of Burgess of Stafford Ltd, was a lorry registered PRE 905, which is a Stafford registration. On one occasion we lost a piston in Wye Street, Ross-on-Wye, which is a very steep hill, about 1 in 5 gradient. The mechanic who was driving it at the time wrote on his time sheet, 'searching for Bradford piston in Wye Street, one and a half hours!' Needless to say the old girl had to have a new engine fitted.

The old Bradford had a tendency to wander on the road, usually when a large lorry was passing. I think it would have been hit several times if it had had another coat of paint on it! The clutch pedal had been used that much a hole was in the floorboards where numerous boot heels had scraped over them. This was not too clever in cold weather I might say!

There were quite a lot of Jowetts in the area in the late 1950s. The Javelin was popular with farmers, also the Bradford Utility. The firm also ran a Bradford van, which was also registered PRE ???, but I cannot remember the number; it was actually based at our depot in Monmouth. The only other little escapade I can tell you about is when the Bradford lorry 'gave up the ghost' going up a steep hill. To be fair on the Bradford, it was only carrying twelve steel field gates, that's all … use and abuse!

David J. Cooper, Ross-on-Wye, Herefordshire

Maurice Slee

I remember my late father, Maurice Slee, driving Bradford vans in the 1950s. He was born in 1912 and died a couple of years ago at the age of eighty-five. He worked for the same employer for over fifty years and learned to drive on a 2-ton truck, long before the days of driving tests.

The fleet of Bradford and Ford vans owned by Rood Brothers Ltd of Southampton. These vans were all a dark green, but were not sign-written. Maurice Slee is third from the left.

A fleet of vans were operated by Rood Brothers Ltd [around 1960], a firm of general wholesalers that was located in a large warehouse in Bevois, Valley Road, Southampton. It was at the time that the company were transferring their allegiance to the new Ford Thames van. My father was the senior salesman (reps or commercial travellers they used to call them in those days) and so had the privilege of making the transition first.

As a boy in the 1950s I remember going to the warehouse on a Saturday morning with dad where I would meet Arthur Rood, one of the four brothers who had carried on the business started by their father. Arthur was a very precise, dapper gentleman who looked after the transport and took great pride in his fleet of Bradfords and other larger Dodge and Ford vans. He insisted that they were regularly washed, cleaned and polished. Another privilege of the senior salesman was that my father always received the newest Bradford. They all had local registrations such as FCR, FTR, JCR and JOW. Looking back it seems curious that none of the Bradfords was sign-written, although all were the same bottle green colour. So proud was Arthur of his fleet that a photograph of it always appeared on at least one of the monthly pages of the company calendars.

The company garage was in Verulum Road, being a few hundred yards from the warehouse. Late on a Saturday morning all the vans were 'at home' for the weekend. In my mind I can still smell that wonderful aroma of warm, burned oil from the twelve Bradfords, which slept snugly behind damp canvas curtains, with their pungent odour, hanging across the entrances. I would help my father fill the petrol tank of his Bradford from an ageing piston pump on one side of the garage yard.

I can still remember the Bradford quite well with its elliptical rear windows and black fabric-covered roof. It carried what I recall a 'C licence', which I believe stood for Commercial, as it was designed to carry just the owners goods. [*Yes the Bradford van was sold with just a driver's seat; the passenger seat was an optional extra! NS*] In my father's case it was the samples of goods that the wholesaler had for sale, which could have been anything from clothes to china or fancy goods to stationary. A further privilege for the senior salesman was to keep his Bradford at home, convenience aside; the privilege was a doubtful one! Dad had the use of the van in the evenings and weekends, but the commercial configuration of the van did not suit my mother and I. For family outings he had padded the top of a wooden box that loose-fitted the space next to the driver, this was to be my mother's seat. I had a 'proper' seat in the back of the van in the form of a seaside deckchair. I think that one misses so much fun in these modern days of seatbelts and airbags!

In the 1950s we had no garage at home and the Bradfords languished on our gravel driveway. On cold or wet nights the van was shrouded in a heavy canvass tarpaulin supplemented with its latest plastic equivalent. The bonnet also had an extra undergarment in the form of a blanket. All these layers were weighed down with bricks attached by string, to stop them flapping in the breeze. The cocoon was completed by a large board leaning against the grille to stop wind blowing into the radiator and under the engine. Is the privilege of the senior salesman now wearing thin?!

Winter months were the most precarious, as the battery never seemed strong enough to turn over the Bradford engine, never mind actually start it! A swing of the starting handle usually did the trick, which was often my job once I was nine or ten years old. I had been taught how to hold the handle so that when the engine fired, it did not break my wrist. The most precarious bit was how we kept the chill off the engine overnight to make early starting rather easier. My father had a small paraffin heater that he placed on a piece of wood balanced between the engine block and the dynamo. Indoors it often got so cold that there was frost inside of the windows, but not in the driveway: the Bradford was as warm as toast with its paraffin heater and tarpaulin covers over the bonnet!

Andrew Slee, Fareham, Hampshire

PML 1

My father bought a new Bradford van in 1949, the first new car he had owned since the war, I was twelve at the time. The registration number was PML 1 and was yellow. It was bought without side windows, to avoid paying purchase tax. My father had three windows put in down each side and two rear ones, one in each door. He also fitted a bench seat in the middle of the rear, this was out of a coach or bus, also two backward facing seats behind this.

These two seats folded flat so he could put luggage on top of them. He was always able to secure a '1' registration as he worked for the vehicle taxation office at the time!

We used the car that summer for our holiday in North Cornwall and the owner of the guest house gave us some of his surplus petrol coupons, so we put them to good use driving all round the area. He kept the Bradford until the spring of 1955, when he sold it to a couple from West London – Harrow Road, I think. They sent us Christmas cards for approximately the next ten years, as they were as pleased with it as we were!

We lived in West Ealing during this period. My father de-cocked the engine twice during these six years of ownership. On both occasions he did this on the kitchen table, and it was during this that I learned in detail how the internal combustion engine worked. I am pleased to say that my mother did not seem to mind!

When I was seventeen he tried to teach me how to drive it, but I just could not master the crash gearbox and double-

The Bradford 6-light, registered PML 1, taken in 1950. It started life in 1949 as a van, owned by Hugh Edwards' father, who is now ninety-three. He had the three windows down each side fitted, to avoid purchase tax.

Hugh Beesley of Carlisle with his Bradford Utility, registered KAO 812, on a camping trip in the 1950s.

declutching, and we both gave up after mutual consent! My dad is now in his ninety-sixth year and still has fond memories of the Bradford.

Hugh Edwards, Reading

A passion for Jowetts

My late father had a passion for Jowetts and bought a Bradford van from a friend in 1959. It had previously been converted with windows in the side and a fancy paint job, it reminded me of a Morris Traveller.

Anyway, we were all comfortable as dad had fitted a couple of old London Transport bus seats in the back. There was just enough room behind them to squeeze in a large Silver Cross pram, together with all the luggage a growing family would need for a fortnight's self-catering holiday in Seasalter.

Not long after dad bought the Bradford it was stolen, but recovered a couple of days later. The police told us it had been used as a getaway car in a bank robbery in Dalston!

The robbers couldn't have had much 'upstairs', as Bradford's were not built for speed; maybe they had heard that Javelins were fast and nimble, got confused, and stole the wrong model of Jowett! Anyway they rolled it in the chase.

My father was not one to let something like this defeat him, so he took it to my uncle's house which had a sideway. He then parked it close to the house wall and, with clever use of jacks, he was able to straighten it out and soon it was as good as new!

Another memorable incident was while on holiday in Seasalter, a couple of years later. After a day out in the Bradford we pulled up outside our chalet when we heard a terrific bang followed by steam and smoke coming from under the bonnet. One of the 'pots' had blown its lid and half the engine was lying on the gravel under the car. Again this did not deter my dad, and with my uncle they found a breakers yard near Whitstable and managed to acquire a Bradford engine. Dad did not have time to fit it while on holiday, so put it in the van together with the pram and luggage and had the whole lot towed back to our home in Holloway. As we did not have a garage he just parked it in the street and fitted it there!

As we were a growing family, when we didn't need the space for the large pram anymore, dad sold the Bradford and went on to the luxury of a Javelin; and what a car that was! But before leaving the Bradford, about a year after dad sold it he saw it advertised in *Exchange & Mart* by the person he sold it to, for sale at £15 or exchange for a fishing rod; he saw the funny side!

We had several Javelins over the next few years. We even had one where a previous owner had fitted an old Austin engine; needless to say this was very under-powered so dad fitted a Javelin engine.

During one trip along the M2, the bonnet flew up at around 70mph on the outside lane, but due to its pointed shape dad could just see ahead to pull safely onto the hard shoulder.

Because of the flat-4 engine, they were quite easy to work on – we did not need pulleys to remove and refit the engine. Just put a trolley jack under the engine, disconnect everything and pull the engine out or push the car backwards. How easy is that? It was so easy that I think dad enjoyed doing it a number of times over the years.

Our last Javelin was a series 3, and this was the one I passed my test in, in 1965. As the little button that held the gear lever in reverse didn't work properly, I had to hold it in manually during my reversing manoeuvres. We had this one right up to about 1970, when I got married. My dad started to get breathing difficulties and couldn't manage to do the maintenance himself any longer.

Colin Dolan, Tilehurst, Reading

Learning to drive

I joined a company of insulation engineers in December 1953 and amongst their fleet of vans and trucks they had a Bradford pickup. It was very much a one-driver vehicle and the driver would load it up with 25-gallon cans of bitumen and away he went each day. Nobody else seemed to drive it but whether this was because it was a temperamental starter, or its somewhat alarming roll, I do not know.

Later by sheer chance I bought myself a Bradford van, in fact I learnt to drive in it. I bought it when there was a lifting of restrictions, so I did not have to have a qualified driver to come out with me. That was in the late 1950s, so it was due to the Suez Crisis.

I was looking for a vehicle to go to and fro to work, as it was a four-mile uphill push-bike ride to get home. It was not an ideal vehicle to learn to drive in as it had rather small rear windows. It was a terror to start; I seem to recall that it had an external starting handle, which I had to feed in and turn it slowly until it met resistance. Then it was a sharp pull up and hope it would start first time. Sadly more often than not it didn't, so I had to disengage the handle or get a clout on the knuckles. I clearly remember that if it did not start after three attempts, I would have to wait a while before trying again.

It had a flat plywood floor, only one seat and a long-gear leafier that waved about all over the place. It had an ash frame and aluminium body. I know that, as I had to replace the driver's side rear door and part of the floor. Fortunately the company had a band saw, as it was a multi-curved shape. I seem to remember it had trafficators, which more than once I broke off negotiating a narrow track down to an off-street parking lot. I used this to save leaving a light on overnight.

Unfortunately the horizontally-opposed engine gave me a lot of valve spring trouble. Why this should happen, I do not know, as

I was non-mechanical and still am! I used to have to take it very frequently to my small local garage, who would replace the broken springs, which were always the same ones.

When the time came to take my test, I borrowed a seat from another van and bolted it to the floor so that the examiner now had somewhere to sit. I don't know who was the most worried, him or me. He had to sit with his knees up under his chin, and for some reason never gave me an emergency stop – probably very wise of him!

The Bradford was a reddish brown and I did some longish drives in it, such as Kent to Yorkshire and Kent to Buckingham, but the worry of springs snapping was always with me. In fact they broke on the Kent to Buckingham trip, with my wife, small child and mother-in-law in the back sitting on a mattress. I was lucky, as this happened on the way back, so we were able to limp home running on one cylinder.

It was on the whole, I suppose, a reasonable buy. I cannot remember what I paid for it, possibly £65, but it served its purpose until I could afford something better. I finally sold it to a farmer who cut the back off and used it to ferry bales of hay to his cattle.

Gordon Knight, Brigg, North Lincolnshire

SMY 562

My father bought new from a London garage, one of the first Jowett Bradford vans produced shortly after the war; it was registered SMY 562. The van only had two seats fitted at the front, so my father fitted a temporary seat at the back for me. This was a leather car seat he took out of an old car.

I took my driving test in the Bradford in March 1948, when I was seventeen. The examiner sat in the passenger seat and my instructor sat on the seat in the back. I cannot remember why he came with us, but I am sure it was not usually done this way. I actually hit the kerb when reversing; I must have hit it quite hard, as my instructor lurched forward out of the rear seat. After

Mrs Kay Christmas sent this photograph of the 1948 Bradford van, registered SMY 562. This was bought new by Kay's father. This picture was taken at Forty-Foot Bank, Benwick, Cambs, in 1949.

this set-back I did it again with no problem; the examiner said it was a difficult manoeuvre due to the limited visibility through the small oval windows in the back doors. Due to this he made allowances for my mistake, and so I passed first time! My instructor was very pleased with me, saying that I was the only person he knew of who had passed the test after making a mistake on the three-point turn, so it must have been my lucky day!

Soon after my test, our doctor visited us with a super brand new Jowett Javelin – he asked me if I would like to drive it, needless to say I accepted his offer. It had the gearchange on the steering column and leather bench seats. It was such a contrast from the Bradford van; it was an experience I will never forget.

I am still driving after fifty-five years and still have a clean licence, which all started with me passing the test in the Bradford. I have been driving VW's for some time now, my present one being a Golf.

Mrs Kay Y. Christmas, Swaffham, Norfolk

A replacement pony

I have been driving for fifty-three years this year [2003] and the first motor we had was a 1935 Jowett van. The throttle pedal was in the middle and the handbrake down the side of the driver's seat; the petrol tank was under the bonnet and had to be dipped with a stick for checking fuel.

My father was a milkman with a pony and milk float, but as the round got very scattered we thought it was time we got a van. I learnt the basics in the Jowett van, then we got chance of a Bradford, the one with the three windows each side. It was first registered in December 1947, but was a 1948 model CB with the downdraught carb but still only with a six-volt battery system.

It took from July 1950 to February 1951 to get through the test (third time lucky). We ran the Bradford for four years and then my father sold the milk round. I got married at this time and kept the Bradford and turned it into a private car. I made a bench seat in the back, making use of the wheel boxes, and it could seat four easily; some carpets down and front seat covers made it quite comfortable.

In 1956 we wanted a different holiday and thought we would try Penzance (friends thought we were mad). Anyway we went – it took two days to get there and two back, which people can't understand today. At this period, after doing the milk round, the van was burning oil. I fitted cord rings later in the year, but at this time the van was only doing fifty miles to the pint. It was a case of carrying plenty of oil and keeping one eye on the milometer! Anyway we made it and the only mishap was a rear light glass was smashed: somebody didn't stop quick enough on the then notorious Exeter bypass! We took the van to Lands End and, to make sure for getting home, we joined the AA there, but we got home without any trouble.

We ran the Bradford for sixteen years, and the only time it let me down and had to be left at the side of the road was after taking a mate back to Leeds station. On the way back home one of the con rods went and smashed the piston through the barrel of the cylinder. After that episode one cylinder bore was different to the other. Well, after a while the body started to rot and my wife thought it was time for a change. A friend who was a decorator took the van and utilised engine spares on the van he was running.

After that I went on to run DAF's which have a similar engine, only air-cooled. I ran DAF's for twenty years, but that's another story…

Frank C. Parkin, Liversedge, West Yorkshire

This is the Bradford owned by Edward Skuce, a fruiterer and greengrocer. The picture is taken outside his shop in Park Road, Hornsey, North London. This picture was sent in by his daughter, Beryl Hayman.

A Greengrocer's Van

My father bought a Jowett Bradford Van in 1949 or '50 and we ran it for many years. After service in the Air Force I joined my father in his business in 1950 and recall driving the van back from Bradford. I remember that it was unlike any other vehicle I had driven – it would go up a house-side in first gear (but first gear could only be engaged from a standing start). It was very economical on petrol, which was an advantage in those post-war years.

My father's business was greengrocery and the van was used to bring fresh vegetables from Leeds market each morning (very early); delivering customer orders etc. He also had a contract with the Local Education Authority for delivery of school meals to five schools in the Morley area from a central kitchen at Gildersome. The size of the van was such that it could hold the large containers (both round and oblong) with ease and there was no lip at the back doors which meant the containers (which were quite heavy) could be slid from the van.

One drawback with the Bradford was the brakes. Being rod brakes they had a bad habit of snapping. I well remember two occasions going down Churwell Hill when the brakes failed and the only way to stop was to run first into the kerb and then scrape along a wall! They once failed while on a visit to a scout camp at Lofthouse. I called the AA and the engineer mended them with a ladies hairclip. It got me home.

Here in Morecambe I recall seeing a Jowett rally some years ago, including the famous Jowett Bradford vans.

Roy and Barbara Chapman, Morecambe

Waltzing Matilda

I bought my Jowett Bradford van at auction, and at the time I thought it was a real snip. As I was in the food retail trade, I fitted it out with due regard to appearance and hygiene considerations. By the time I had finished she was as pretty as a picture!

It was a great little workhorse, but it had a mind of its own – my children christened it 'Waltzing Matilda', as when it reached 40mph it would drift! On trips to the seaside with the wife and two children on board, we would just manage to stutter to the top of Garrowby Hill, then we would be on our way again OK. [*This would lead you to Bridlington etc., NS*]

I kept this van immaculate; so much so, a local butcher asked me if I would consider doing a straight swap – my Bradford for his Commer shooting-brake – as this was a bit big for his deliveries. The deal was for 'as they stood', so, with all the 'honesty' and business acumen of a Romany horse trader, I allowed him to twist my arm and submitted.

Soon after he quietly said to me that he had to 'get rid' of Matilda due to mechanical problems. After a few years I traded the Commer in with a 'sharp' Cockney roadside car sales outfit, bemoaning the fact that he had done the deal with a 'slow-speaking Yorkshire lad', as he described its shortcomings!

In spite of numerous cars over the years since, even now the kids (youngest aged fifty-two) still have a laugh about the fun we had going for trips in our old friend Matilda.

Fred Robertson, Addingham, Ilkley

FKY 59

My father came back from the Far East at the end of the Second World War, late like most of his fellow airman, to find that all the promises of safe work had vanished and that he was left with nothing.

After some hard times he got a job as a traveller in the East Midlands with a Leeds-based ladies gown and coat company called Marldina. We moved to Nottingham and they provided him with a Bradford van the registration of which was FKY 59, and the colour I recall was sand or beige, whichever you prefer! We were very lucky – not much money – but a small house in the country just outside Nottingham and a car – something that not many people had in those days.

We did so much and had some wonderful family times – life in Nottingham was great – I am certain that the old Bradford had a lot

to do with it. Dad got the chance to buy our rented house but could not afford the deposit that would have been required for the £1,000 mortgage. The company transferred him to its sister company, Marlbeck, and we had to move to South London, where he travelled the South East of England.

He ran the Bradford between 1947 and possibly 1952. It was second-hand when given to him, so by the time it went back to Leeds I cannot image what miles it had on the clock because he travelled far each day. Where the vehicle went after its return to Leeds I have no idea. Our next vehicle was an Austin – possibly A60 – purpose-built Gown van registered RUB 63, I think.

Tim Potts, Grantham, Lincs

GBM 10

Perhaps from my youth my one regret was that I didn't have the cash or the foresight to retain my Bradford van, my first car. My brother and I both had Bradfords, his was a '48 I think, which was registered GBM 10, bought from Bedford Auction sometime around Winter 1961/62.

We both were practical nuts for anything mechanical and did virtually everything ourselves, much to the surprise of our parents. My brother, having paid £9 for it, got it home four miles to discover both barrels cracked from frost. If only after opening them we had checked the taps were clear with a wire after it had run in the auction yard. Anyway with repeated use of Radweld they steadied up and, so long as water was with us, we never had any problems. I think the engine front main bearing was moving in the crankcase when he bought it, so with a new bearing, also a shade loose, we then cured the problem with araldite and mother's kitchen oven! I don't recall when he sold it or where it went, but he traded up to a Citroen 2CV, 375cc with all of 9bhp.

My Bradford, a 1952/53 I believe, was registered FBL 355 was bought for £15 from a garage in Bromham Road, Bedford, probably in 1962 when I was seventeen. It was a choice between that or a Bond Minicar! It too had cracked barrel problems but not from us, these had been welded reasonably. It had windows in the rear with an ex-trolley bus seat installed between the mudguards. It was altogether the better of the two and, after attention to all the brake rod clevis ends, could stop extremely well. Mine went for £22 10s about a year later to someone who drove it back up to Ilkley, I recall.

I moved on to a Fiat Topolino with a seized engine! I recall that my mother at some time stored a Jowett 8hp in our garden for someone. Dad always told us that the Javelin was way ahead of its time, and [we] longed to find one in our youth, but I guess it was cash flow then. My recollections were recently stirred seeing the Bradford ice cream van in Hull's Museum of Town Life.

W.D. Basford, Southwell, Notts

Rabotnik

In 1957/58 we were living in London and couldn't afford a car. On the birth of our first child we had an income tax rebate of £75 which we used to buy a second-hand Bradford van. We called it 'Rabotnik', which is Russian for worker, because Sputnik was in the news about then. Unfortunately the front-end bearing was leaking oil, [so] I went to a garage in Harrow (I think the name was Buntings). I couldn't afford to have the garage fix it, as I was a student. They took pity on me and gave me a space in the garage and instructed me how to fix it – and I only had to pay for the cost of spares. They were absolutely fantastic.

Douglas Owen, Croyde, Devon

A Hairpin

After we bought the van, my husband went to start a new job in the Potteries. He went on ahead to arrange accommodation, and I followed with the van a little later. Our daughter was asleep in her pram, which was wedged among the luggage in the back of the van. We were well out of London, on a

The ferry to the Continent, 1950s fashion! This picture shows the Bradford Utility registered CJN 263 being hoisted aboard.

country road far from any telephone, when the accelerator suddenly refused to work. The pedal went up and down with no resistance. I stopped the van on the grass verge and got out. I knew nothing about car engines, but I managed to open the bonnet and looked inside. After some poking about, I found what was obviously the two pieces of a broken chain. One end vanished into the engine, and the other appeared to be attached to the accelerator pedal. I joined the two broken ends together with a hairpin, and found, to my delight, that the accelerator now worked perfectly. By the time I had driven the remaining fifty to sixty miles to my destination, I had forgotten about the hairpin. My husband found it, to his surprise, some time later when he had occasion to open the bonnet (to check the oil, perhaps). They don't make vans like that nowadays, or hairpins either!

Ann Owen, Croyde, Devon

[*I enjoyed these two letters, as both Mr and Mrs Owen took the trouble to write to me. NS*]

'...and a dash...'

My father, who had a shop in Park Road, Hornsey, North London, owned a Jowett Bradford van.

If I remember correctly it was light brown, and the back opened in two, divided horizontally. He used it continually to go to Spitfield's Market, also for light removals, and for us, a great deal of pleasure – including picnics on Sundays! We had orange boxes to sit on down each side in the back. On a hot day we would open the top back window while on our journey, which would cool us down. There were always two deck chairs in the back of the van for mum and dad; my brother, twin sister and I (plus cocker spaniel) were left to roam in the fields, paddle in brooks and generally appreciate the delights of the countryside, in contrast to busy London.

I also remember that it had a starting handle, but I am not sure if it also had a self-starter as well. [*Yes it would have had one. NS*] It was never kept in a garage, but was always reliable in all weathers. I also remember when he filled up with petrol, he would also say, 'and a dash' (this referred to a shot of Reddex – this was upper cylinder lubricant, so my husband tells me!)

Mrs Beryl Hayman, Wheathampstead, Herts

[*This letter was of particular interest to me as the Bradford that Beryl's father had, had back doors that opened in two halves, horizontally. The production Bradford had two opening back doors, which opened vertically. This van must, therefore, have had these made to special order. NS*]

A flying Jowett

I was employed by a brewery in Sheffield, and drove a Ford 8 van, this was written off in an accident, so I was in need of new transport. The only vehicle that my management were able to find me in the pool of vehicles was an ancient 8hp Jowett van.

Now the Army teaches you to always check for yourself things like fuel, oil and water levels – so as to not find yourself embarrassed after driving away in the thing. Seemingly this philosophy had been handed down to many others – particularly in the lubricating oil department. This particular Jowett did not have a dipstick for checking the oil, rather a sort of float arrangement that in theory had markings on it indicating the level of oil: as an Irish gent might have said 'to be sure'. All this 'to be sure' of course led to an overfull sump. The vehicle sullenly refused to start until it had been milked of some of the excessive oil that had been blocking its pores, so to speak. Even then a tow was required, and eventually when she fired up, the resulting smoke cloud was something to see – it almost obscured the brewery premises! So for a few days I put-tered about in this thing, and indeed 'putter' was the descriptive word to describe the sound it made, being a flat-twin engine.

Then something straight from a comedy script happened, which I guess had a bearing on my future mode of transport. I was instructed to meet my boss, Miss A.S. Hart, from Victoria Station, Sheffield, and transport her to the brewery, as on this occasion she had commuted by train. Miss Hart was the first lady boss I had worked for; she must have been one of the few executive ladies around at the time. There was no doubt she was an extremely able and intelligent woman! She had an abiding passion for sport and saw this area as a terrific medium for advertising; she was indeed the brewery's Advertising Manager! Amongst her many attributes was a Directorship of the famous Belle View entertainment complex in Manchester. She was also the only female holder of a Speedway Promoters Licence in the coun-try, at a time when Speedway had a tremendous following. Her personal kindness to me was immense, but that's another story!

However I duly picked up 'The Boss' and set off in the Jowett. At a set of lights, not quite having mastered the temperamental clutch, we lurched forward in a somewhat hasty manner. I was shocked to see 'the gov-ernor's' seat hurtle backwards, as it was unsecured to the flooring (I then discov-ered). This gave me an impressive view of my leader's legs and underwear – at a time when these things were not on general view to the staff (as it were!). Having assisted in the restoration of decorum and suitable grav-ity, we drove to the brewery in silence. Would I ever be forgiven? I'm glad to say I was, eventually, but the event speeded-up my next 'work' vehicle. It turned out to be another Jowett, this time a much newer Bradford van. This one was quite smart, a dark green colour, but strangely enough

with no brewery logo. Over time I began to love and admire this little van, but needless to say many little adventures were to come my way whilst I was driving it.

So, accustoming myself with the Jowett marque, which seemed to be mine for the foreseeable future, I carried on with my dis-play work, moving around the countryside as in the days of yore. The Jowett was, I think, registered OWJ 55; it was not as nippy as the Ford, but was robust and built like a tank! Again there was no heater, a com-monplace situation then, but it did have proper windscreen wipers and was electric motor driven.

I frequently did display work inside work-ing men's clubs, brightening up dingy bar areas, showcases etc. How many can boast, as I did quite frequently then, that I had spent the day working in The Idle Working Men's Club! As you know, Jowetts were built in Idle, Bradford, so there must have been Jowett workers inside.

On an icy morning I was in a line of traf-fic waiting at a set of temporary traffic lights at some road works. A new (very chic) and expensive Ford Zephyr came tanking up, but could not stop and ploughed into me, caus-ing a massive shunt as we all ploughed into each other. It was just like a 'Direct Line TV advert' – all those car numbers to take! The instigator, having given his details, fled to the nearest garage, as his designer front end had been well and truly mangled, and had anti-freeze pouring all over the place. Such was the rugged nature of the Bradford, all I had sustained was a large dent in one of the rear doors. The front end, thanks to the strong front bumper, wasn't even scratched.

Eventually the van went in for repairs to the door, which still locked despite the distortion. The garage doing the repairs were anxious to get more work from the brewery so took care of one or two minor dents at the same time. The wings had also been repainted, so when it came back it looked like a new vehicle. Soon after this I 'lost' one of the cylinders, I am not sure why, but probably [through] a burnt-out valve. She ran for several months like this, with very little drop in performance, except on hills – some engine!

The engine did finally die on me, but manifested some strange warnings before the main bearings went. The dipstick, which thought itself a torpedo, leaped out of its housing at regular intervals, with a loud clang! A new engine was required and was fitted by a local Jowett agent.

All was going well with the Bradford, but one day I got stuck in top gear. I had left the trunk road and was following a long, winding lane, running downhill. I was hoping I would be able to dislodge it from the top position, but it was well and truly jammed! Needless to say the lane led me to a quaint country pub, which seemed to be the ideal place to ring for help. I spoke to the brewery. Telling them my tale of woe, so the breakdown boys were sent to help me. It took them a long time to find me from the directions I had given them, but find me they did, and towed me back to the brewery garage for some remedial treatment. I thought afterwards that if you are going to get stranded, a nice little country pub is the place to do it at!

Another adventure I had in the Bradford happened soon after, and once again showed the rugged nature of the beast! In Sheffield at that time was a large brick and tile works, whose factory was at a place called Stannington. On the site of its works was a social club building of quite an impressive size. I visited here from time to time to dress the bar shelves and other areas. However, on my first visit I had arrived by daylight, but left in the darkness of a winter's afternoon. The road to the club was narrow and winding, the clubhouse standing on a slight rise. After my display session I started up the Bradford and

saw that the exit road seemingly lay straight in front of me, as I set off from the tiny car park. Wrong! The road that appeared before me in the dim headlights was a continuation of the approach road, and was in fact well below me, as I was about to find out. In reality it lay a good 6–8ft below me as I set off. Seeing too late what I was about to do, I braked hard. It was like a dream in slow motion as we gently went nose first over the drop. With great dignity the old girl slowly toppled over, seemingly landing with just a little bump. I was stranded in mid-air with the front wheels on the narrow road below and the back wheels still firmly ensconced on a level with the club car park above!

Having climbed out and then down (with some difficulty) plus being somewhat panic-stricken, I made my way to a well-lit workshop of some sort. There were a number of men hard at work inside. Stammering out my problem, laced with 'Can you help me?'s, I was amazed to see them falling about in laughter, the foreman saying something on the lines of 'Nobody's done that for ages son! It cheers us up no end when they do', which was followed by more hearty laughter. But they then all downed their tools and followed me out to see my predicament. Somehow getting me back into the driver's seat, they then hoisted me up, and the team on top pulled me back onto terra firma. Their kindness then continued by directing me to the works garage. Here mechanics, between gales of laughter, checked the van over. The only damage I had sustained, believe it or not, was that I had 'squared off' the underside of the originally rounded silencer! I was very relieved to see I had not even split it. I had no accident report to fill in to lay before our traffic manager – phew, what a relief.

Old men from Stannington probably still recollect the event to this day, over their cups of tea, on the lines of, 'Dos't remember yon daft bugger who tried to drive off from

This Bradford Utility, registered PTE 708, was owned by Trevor Hartley in 1969. The picture was taken on a trip to Scotland in 1969. I bought this Bradford in April 2001 and have had a lot of fun with it since.

t' club that time, thinking his old Jowett had wings? Silly twit!'

So the Bradford and I soldiered on for many more months with nothing to report in terms of motoring interest. When the Jowett was in for servicing, I was loaned a much newer 10hp Ford Thames van from the dispatch department. The difference the extra two horses made was very noticeable, so I yearned to have one of my own. Later on I did, but that is another story which I will not tell here!

Leslie Ives, Bishopsmead, Tavistock, Devon

PTE 708

I bought PTE 708, a Bradford Utility (and a second one in very poor condition) in 1968 in Leyland, Lancs. I paid £30 for them and that included a box of new spares; I subsequently sold these for £40 – not a bad deal!

Bradfords in those days seemed to appear in pairs, as I had just previously bought another pair for £10. I had started restoring one of them, but found serious corrosion in the chassis and scrapped it.

PTE was the best of the four, and I got it running and MOT'd early in 1969. At that time standards were a bit more lax; one of the semaphore trafficators was on the back seat when the test was carried out!

I took two friends on a tour of Scotland in the summer of 1969 – Halifax to Edinburgh, Kinross, Glasgow, Dumfies and back to Halifax – accompanied by many punctures and frequent failures of the back lights, which earthed on the exhaust pipe! The exhaust finally collapsed and had to be repaired. The body frame was poor and we had the back doors tied up with string on the last stages of the journey.

I went to university in September 1969, so I passed it on to a friend in Halifax who ran it for a while. I have enjoyed jotting these memories, and enjoyed PTE. I later ran a 1934 Jowett 7 for twelve years.

Trevor Hartley, Stourbridge, West Midlands

[*This Bradford had changed hands several times before it was restored. I am pleased to say I bought it in April 2001. NS*]

it takes 4 drivers

For an expert driver it can be tough being a passenger.

Back-seat-driving; when your foot comes down hard on the floor boards and you have to hold on to yourself not to sing out.

But here, thank goodness, is a car that's built to take a driver in every seat and keep him happy. You cannot help feeling the absolute *safety* of the car — its iron grip of the road, the masterful way it has with corners and the fine indifference with which it treats the hills.

Yes, here you sit in the back actually enjoying it. And suddenly you're surprised that you can stretch your legs — long though they are. And you can loll about as you like. There's such a lot of room.

Then you remember — what someone once told you — you get more body room because that hyper-efficient engine is so compact, so far forward. And so here you are gliding

along ahead of the back axle with the torsion bar suspension soaking up the bumps and the clock showing a steady cruising 70.

You puff a cigarette and offer one to the other fellow. Hello! — he's watching the scenery. What a car this is — two back-seat-drivers not bothering to drive.

This car is a waste of money if you don't care what a car does. There's such a lot built into it that doesn't really show until you have it in your hands. Once tried, you'll say 'I'd rather go by Javelin!'

Top speed, electrically timed, 78 m.p.h. Acceleration 0-60 m.p.h. in 22.2 secs. ("*The Motor*" Road Test)

Horizontally opposed flat-four 50 B.H.P. engine.

Javelin Saloon : £595
    plus purchase tax £166.0.7.
Javelin Saloon de luxe : £695
    plus purchase tax £193.16.1.

There are over 200 fully qualified Service Agents in Great Britain.

1½ LITRE

.JAVELIN

take a good look when it passes you

JOWETT CARS LIMITED, IDLE, BRADFORD.   48, ALBEMARLE STREET, PICCADILLY, W.1

3 The Javelin
Take a good look when it passes you!

Grille and bonnet

I owned a Javelin in 1960–61, at that time owners carried out most of their own maintenance. I was lucky as I was in the engineering trade, so was able to get parts made if they were not available from Jowett Engineering Ltd at Howden Clough, Birstall. In those days I lived in Batley and was a car fanatic, so spent all my time polishing the heads and timing the engine.

On one occasion I'd been timing the carb's and, as usual, the best way to work on the engine was to remove the grille and bonnet. I lived in Carlinghow Lane at the time; it had an incline about one mile long and I used it as my timed run to test the car after I had worked on it. There were no houses on this road at the time, and I could not be bothered to put the grille and bonnet back on, so off I went to do my timed trial.

As luck would have it, I turned round at the top as a police car was passing by. It turned down the road and tried to catch me. When I pulled into the drive the police car pulled up, and I thought I'd had it! Yes, the policemen were interested in the speed I was doing, but were more interested in the car! Over tea we discussed the engine and suspension, and only on leaving did they just mention that it was against the law to drive without a grille and bonnet on!

It was a lot of years before I had a car that could match the speed and performance of that car.

Derrick Blacker, Cleethorpes, N.E. Lincs

MYH 770

In 1954 I purchased my Javelin, a 1949 model coloured green and registered MYH 770, from 'Clarkes of Pirbright', the main Jowett agent in Pirbright, Surrey. It was on the market as the previous owner, a colonel in the Army stationed in Aldershot, had been killed in the Barnes rail crash.

It was a beautiful car and was one of the delights of my life. It was interesting as behind the dashboard seals from the Monte Carlo Rally were still in place.

One of the faults of the engine was the necessity to keep the two carburettors synchronized to obtain an even tick-over, and carburettor adjustment was, and is still, not one of my skills.

I kept the car for approximately three years when I was seduced to sell it to purchase an Austin A90, which certainly did not have the looks or flair of the Javelin. In particular the column gear change was rubbish compared to the excellent Javelin.

It was a distinguishable car of which there are very few today. My current car is a Jaguar XJ6, which I have had since new, and am loath to part with.

But I have to say no modern car will give me the pleasure I had when I first sat in the Javelin almost fifty years ago.

Ralph Matthews, Woking, Surrey

A nice shot of a Javelin, registered WRF 90, filling up with petrol, 1950s style. This picture was donated to the Jowett Car Club library by club member John Priest.

HBT 483

My late father, Arthur Mendham, owned a Jowett Javelin from approximately 1955 to 1962, he lived in Hull. I think the car was a 1948 example but I cannot be totally sure, it was registered HBT 483. This was his first car and was his absolute pride and joy. During the time that he owned it much of his spare time was spent tinkering with the engine and of course cleaning and polishing it!

Every summer we travelled from Hull to Plymouth to spend our holidays with my grandparents. This journey usually took twelve hours. In 1962, however, our usual twelve hours took twenty-seven hours! The car started overheating within a short distance from home, which necessitated us stopping, waiting for the engine to cool and then refilling with water. My parents decided to soldier on and, as I recall, this process had to be repeated every ten miles or so.

Somewhere near Exeter we had to go up a very steep hill, which I think was called Haldon Hill. It was at this point my father thought he would have to admit defeat. The garage at the bottom of the hill, however, managed to temporarily sort out the problem, so we made it to Plymouth! I believe that our holiday money and much more was spent trying to sort out the fault. We did return to Hull after the holiday without any further hitches.

After this memorable holiday my parents reluctantly decided they could no longer afford to run the Javelin and part exchanged it for a Ford Anglia! My mother remembers the car being put on display on the garage forecourt for all to admire. As to the fate of our dear old car after that, we have no idea.

Mrs Jill Hart, North Ferriby, East Yorkshire

LLG 552 and CGR 961

I no longer have much paperwork concerning my Javelin ownership but I can still recall the enjoyable years of motoring, which included servicing and repairing, they provided me with.

My first Javelin was an early (possibly 1949) model, registration no. LLG 552, which I bought in November 1957 and ran until May 1963. It had, I believe, originally been 'Golden Sand' coloured but was black when I bought it. It suffered from some considerable rust damage in the front floor area and I had to remove the disintegrating sections. My repairs [also] included hand-making and fitting front door sills. In the end I gave up the unequal struggle against rust and broke up the car altogether.

My second Javelin was registered CGR 961 and was, I believe, a 1953 model in metallic green which I bought in August 1962 from a private owner in Sunderland, who had had the car professionally maintained by a firm in Yorkshire. It served me

well until about mid-1968 when I sold it, together with the spare engine from LLG 552, to someone living in Rotherham, S. Yorks. (for I think £22 10s 0d). I used the car on a camping trip carrying four adults, three children and full camping kit for two weeks.

I have many happy memories of my days with my Javelins.

Mr V. Harrison, Horsforth, Leeds

KLR 140

I was a traffic policeman in the early 1950s, operating on the A23 London to Brighton Road. A garage owner who used to help us with accidents asked me one day if I was interested in a car to renovate and repair via his resources; i.e. trade engineers etc. He showed me the car (I had never heard of Jowett Javelins). Apparently it had been neglected in every way, mechanical and body.

The son of the owner was driving to Brighton the previous evening from London

Two very early Javelins in Millard's Garage showroom, Guernsey, in 1948. Theo Millard and his son, John, are with the cars. Registration number 5729 is chassis number 209, and 5777 is chassis number 213. In all, only fourteen Javelins were exported to Guernsey.

and the engine had blown-up through lack of oil. The con rods had done their work by going through the block etc. – a lot of damage. I was told what would be needed in the way of spares and repairs etc. I gave him about £100 and from then on I was on my own, with his help re trade spares and repairs.

The case was badly damaged and needed specialist welding as it was aluminium, but eventually I repaired and reassembled the engine and restored the bodywork. Both off-side doors were badly rusted. As silly as it may seem, the body interior was perfect after a clean. The tools were still in the boot tray untouched and there was even a manual and brochure in the car. It took me a long time, money permitting, to restore the car but the engine was easy to remove.

I had several years of luxury motoring, which included a trip on the Continent via the St Gotthard Pass (the [Channel] tunnel wasn't thought of then) to Italy and the Low Countries – you name it, the car went there!

The car was a 1949-example registered KLR 140, and I must have had it for six or seven years. It sure was a car ahead of its time,

bearing in mind the futuristic engine design (fan at the back, etc.), suspension and comfortable interior.

H. Covington, Birchwood, Lincoln

SPL 323 – a 'real' car!

During the war years my father worked at Hackbridge Cables near Wallington in Surrey as an electrical engineer building tanks. I remember him selling his trusty 'Flying Standard 9' in which we had had many eventful holidays in Devon and Cornwall. On retirement he treated himself to a beautiful streamlined Jowett Javelin which was registered SPL 323. It was coloured Golden Sand and a real step-up in luxury; he referred to it as his 'real' car!

He used to spend a lot of time walking round it thumping the wings with his fist, to demonstrate to me and the neighbours how solid the build quality was. At that time my dream car was a Bristol sports car, but when the Jowett Jupiter hit the showrooms my heart was lost. Class, Style and Sex all in one go!

The Javelin owned by Ronnie Barker's father, registered SPL 323. In 1959 Ronnie bought a Mini and his father had a field day comparing his real car to Ronnie's cake tin!

A nice happy family group with their Javelin in Geneva.

Unfortunately, by the time I had finished my national service in 1959, and was ready to purchase my first car, the market was besotted with the new Mini, so I bought one. With the Mini's carpets regularly hanging on the line to dry and its various problems (petrol pump failing before I had even run it in, the gear stick 'set in concrete' and the distributor soaking up the rain), my father really had a field day comparing my modern 'cake tin' to his 'real' car.

There is not much else to write about his car, because he had years of trouble-free motoring in it, although he did comment that it was difficult to change the plugs, as they were hard to get to.

Ronnie Barker, Worthing

TNU 984

I owned a Jowett Javelin registered TNU 984, which was a dark green metallic colour, for a short time between 1958 and 1959. It was a 1953 model, which I bought from Scarborough prior to coming to Cambridge as a young vet starting off in his own practice.

Unfortunately Cambridge experienced one of its few snowy winters, and I had more than a few problems with the car in slush and snow on the road. On one occasion I was called out to a calving and it had started to snow. I ended the eight-mile trip running on two cylinders. By the end of the calving the car had dried out but the wet conditions soon affected the car again and I just managed to limp home!

Les Kirkbride, Cambridge

DFK 595

My husband and I had a Javelin in November 1949, when we lived in Worcester. It was turquoise and registered DFK 595. We really loved that car, and no other car we have had since has had the same thrill as that one.

We kept the car for five years, but after the closure of Jowett Cars Ltd in 1954 my husband was worried that obtaining spares might become difficult to obtain, so decided to sell the Javelin.

We bought a Vauxhall Velox and I never liked that car after having the Javelin, I could have wept when I watched a man drive away in our Jowett!

Mrs Marjorie Dovey, Bournemouth

Self-service

Although I am now eighty-two years old, my owning of both a Jupiter and Javelin fifty years ago, particularly the Javelin, which I retained for four years, are vivid in my memory. Perhaps the most outstanding feature on both cars was the steering column gearchange, the travel was short and very concise.

The small table that clipped on the back of the front seat of the Javelin was a great asset to my three-year-old daughter, who stood in the back playing on it. On one occasion I drove from Pinner to Caister-on-Sea, a distance of 143 miles, and she stood and played the whole way! A good example of the car's excellent ride and stability provided by the torsion bar suspension.

Being able to do my own servicing added to the pleasure of car ownership, and I can still relate some of the conditions I dealt with. The most serious was the vaporizing of petrol in the induction pipe in hot weather. At the advice of Jowett Cars in Bradford, both the Zenith carburettors were replaced, at no cost to me. On one occasion the cooling fan shaft moved out of line; this was no problem, but I had to grind down the thickness of two spanners because of the thin locknuts. The service manual described making a castor cradle for engine removal, which I made up. It was great, and the whole engine and gearbox could be wheeled out in twenty-five minutes.

C.E. Lovejoy, Christchurch, Dorset

LTC 123

Some fifty years ago I was the proud owner of a Jowett Javelin. From 1948 to 1950 I was practising law in St Annes-on-Sea. In 1949 a client, Bob Ellison, who had been in the Monte Carlo Rally, was in the office and said

A nice period garage forecourt shot of a Javelin after servicing, at the Jowett main agents in Hereford, Marriots. The picture was donated to the club many years ago by Keith James.

he was taking delivery of a couple of Javelins and would I be interested? I said I would and, although difficult, I managed to raise the money, the princely sum of £761.

Three things in particular I liked about the car: its quiet engine, the level floor and the front bench seat.

In 1950 my wife and I with three small children moved to Leeds when I took up a legal appointment with Montaque Burton's at their head office in Hudson Road.

Unfortunately, after a year or so, my wife began to complain that we were running a car when money was required to buy new clothes for the children, who were, of course, growing bigger all the time.

One morning I had a puncture near a garage on Roundhay Road. When the owner saw the Javelin he said he was keen on acquiring one and would I take £950? In the circumstances I decided this was the opportunity I needed. I have never again made a profit on a car.

The Javelin's registration number was LTC 123, a Lancashire county number and was easy to remember.

Laurence N. Leach, Blackpool

Pollards Garage

I never owned a Javelin myself, but I was in charge of all spares for the Bradford van, Javelin saloon and the Jupiter sports car at Pollards Garage, Falmouth, the main Jowett agents in Cornwall.

What a wonderful car the Javelin was, and ahead of its time; we sold a lot to local farmers. Jack Pollard was from a farming family, and they were delighted with them, they even used them to drive through the fields! When they came in for servicing they had to be washed before they could be worked on.

I believe we only sold two Jupiters, one to the son of the owners of the then 'Red Line Shoe Company'. As soon as he got the car

he stripped down the engine and set about 'hotting it up' by polishing the heads etc.

The Bradford van was also a very popular vehicle in this area. As you know, it had a flat-twin engine. The local Co-op milk department in Camborne ran a fleet of them.

Back to the Javelin; if my memory serves me well, they stopped buying the Meadows gearbox and started making their own. They then developed a problem: a washer was prone to break and seize the box. I remember packing them up to send them back to Jowett by rail. I think this was a very large nail in their coffin, what a shame. Another problem used to be the main bearings, and the big end bearings in particular.

I used to see a Javelin in Falmouth up to a few years ago, but sadly no more. I also saw a Jupiter in a motorway service station recently, what a lovely looking vehicle.

It was a happy time for me, working on Jowett Cars. Sadly Mr Jack Pollard, his wife and son are dead; his daughter, Jane, is in a nursing home after having a major stroke. Pollards Garage is now a tyre-fit depot, how times change!

Vic Bayliss, Penryn, Cornwall

MLW 676

My own Javelin-owning days are long over, ending as far back as 1962, but my interest in the marque has not died. I still remember reading the *Motor* and *Autocar* road tests on the Javelin in the spring of 1947. I was working abroad, but, as a Bradfordian, I was excited that a product from Bradford had the makings of a world-beater. The list of innovations was so impressive: flat-four engine, flat floor, steering column gear change, curved windscreen, transparent roof panel (though it never saw production), torsion bar suspension — it was all brand new and radical. My family had never owned a car, nor seemed likely to — but dreaming was cheap!

When I returned to England, I taught for a time in Halifax and in 1950 I arranged for a party of my pupils to be taken round the Jowett works in Idle *(in Idle they're never idle!)*. That was fascinating – the only car factory I have ever been in, and I suppose awfully primitive by the standards of modern manufacturers. There was a real hum in the air and a feeling that Jowett was going places. There were even exports and I remember how struck I was by the apparent small size of the CKD boxes, thinking 'there's a whole Javelin in there!' I'm sure I recall also having pointed out to us a blackboard with output figures marked on it – 232 cars – but I do not know how many days that covered.

Anyhow, when I acquired a used 1951 Javelin (MLW 676) in late 1955, I felt I had arrived! We ran the car for 80,000 miles and had a huge amount of pleasure from it, but, towards the end, unreliability, and even breakdowns, forced us to part with it. My wife was as sad as I was, for she had taken her driving test in it in 1956. It was a grand car for a lady driver in those days.

John Cooper, Cheam, Surrey

[*NB. I wrote to John to ask for permission to use his letter in this book in November 2002. His daughter, Helen Marquard, told me he was delighted that I wanted to use his letter. Sadly Helen told me he never got round to writing to me before the cancer he was struggling with took its final hold and he died in December 2002. Helen felt it was fitting for his letter to be used. I am most grateful to Helen and would like to send my condolences to her and her family. NS*]

My Javelin, registered FFR 900, in a 'period' location. I have used similar shots many times when I send my requests for Jowett information to magazine editors. I have to say, it has worked very well over the years!

A saloon car race

I've been in the motor trade all my life, starting my first job at an automobile electrical repair company as a trainee. Just after my twentieth birthday I was called up and became a Craftsman Electrician (V&P) in the REME. After basic training I was posted to No.9 Central Workshops, Bicester, Oxon. On a regiment weekend after a special parade, (whose significance I cannot recall) a bunch of squaddies had arranged with a local coach firm to take us to the Grand Prix meeting at the nearby Silverstone Motor Racing Circuit. A supporting race was a Saloon Car race, which turned out to be very exciting. The race consisted of a range of different groups of competitors from the exotic Jaguars, Aston Martins and Healeys etc. through Javelins down to the humble Morris Minors. They were all racing together on the track with the final results having to be worked out by lapscorers at the end of the race.

This was the most amazing race we watched, seeing Javelins and even tiny Minors out-cornering the larger Jags and other expensive machines. Once on the straights they were just left behind as the more powerful motors continued to amass extra laps. Knowing what I have learnt since then, I think that the torsion bar front suspension on both the Javelin and Minor really allowed them to mix it on the track with the big boys. I wonder what effect modern radial tyres of today's suppliers would have had, if they were available to them then!

The later GP race had to be stopped after several laps due to a violent rainstorm, which caused flooding on a corner where we were watching. The marshals had to stand ankle-deep in water in the middle of the racing line to direct the drivers to shallower parts of the track, before they were able to stop the race. In those days, of course, there was no television or mobile phones, I think it was 1951.

Our fun was not over yet! As we squaddies left in our old Bedford bus we cheered hilariously as a posh new coach in front of us, filled with smart, best-suited young Airmen, had to get out and push their coach, which kept getting stuck in the mud. Our old bus and gentle driver just kept rolling steadily, no foot on the boards for him!

Some years later, my dad bought a second-hand Javelin, which he kept for many years. I did not drive it myself, as now I was married and living away from home. My dad and mom were on holiday near Tenby and he fell and broke his kneecap, and ended up in hospital. We visited him there and it was decided that the hospital would arrange for dad to be transported to our local Warwick hospital to continue his treatment there, mom travelled with him in the ambulance. I drove with a driver to the holiday address to collect the Javelin and bring it home for dad to use as soon as he was able. I found it a beautiful car to drive and was surprised at its cornering ability, but was concerned at the squealing tyres as I set off through the narrow lanes around Saundersfoot. I soon got used to it, and when I looked down at the speedometer I realised why the tyres were squealing. At the time I was driving a 1937 Hillman Minx of about 1100cc side-valve engine and it didn't go like that!

In the late 1950s I worked in a little village garage and a customer brought in a Javelin deluxe with a gearbox problem. These jobs were usually done by the gaffer, but on this occasion he was busy so I did it. I had not done one before but, after the gearbox removal, I stripped it down and rebuilt it with new parts, as needed. I refitted it and was delighted that it went away working perfectly.

Peter L. Horrocks, Henley-in-Arden, Solihull

ONW 888

I lived in Bradford until we moved to Sidcup in Kent to work in London. We had four children and left a large circle of family and friends. As a result we made many return trips to my brother and my Uncle Irving in Shelf, Halifax; our wives were sisters.

Somewhere in my early consciousness I became aware that Jowetts were of special interest locally. That could have been because in the congregation of the Brownroyd Primitive Methodist Chapel, were the Grimley family. They were Mr and Mrs Grimley, a daughter and two sons. One son was Horace and for a couple of years he was my Sunday school teacher, this would have been 1927 or 1928. I have an abiding memory of the ride he gave us in his two-seater Jowett car. Horace was related to the Jowett family and worked at Jowetts right up to the closure of the company in 1954.

In 1957 I bought a Javelin from Uncle Irving, after we had been on holiday with him in the car. We replaced it in 1967 but by then it was a combination of three cars. Over the years I broke two of them up and single-handedly carted them to the Erith dump. The first car was registered ONW 888.

No family got more pleasure from family transport than we did from the dear old Javelin; it was a moving extension of our home. After an outing, to a picnic or the like, coming back to the Javelin and just seeing it in the car park gave us pleasure. Following as it did a 1938 Ford 10, which we had owned since 1949, the Javelin was a Rolls-Royce!

I had rebuilt the Ford on a new chassis, which cost me £12 10s. It was without heating, had a six-volt battery, minimal boot space, a vacuum-driven windscreen wiper, rod brakes and was cramped for four adults. In contrast, the Javelin had everything: fan heater, seal-beam headlights, twelve-volt electrics, column gearchange (whatever made designers go off these?), hydraulic brakes, centre armrest three-seater front

David Flack carrying out running repairs on his Javelin, registered LNG 30; just what you needed when you were on a camping holiday!

bench seat, leather upholstery and a good turn of speed.

Our first trip north in the Ford took ten hours; the Javelin reduced this to less than six. This occasioned the famous expression from Uncle Irving, 'could you just drive round the block' as we arrived in Shelf two hours or so before expected and he was not ready for us!

In the ten years with our Javelin we must have motored about 100,000 miles and we never had to call for roadside assistance. We had quite a few problems but always managed to cure them one way or another. We rarely went far without our toolkit, plus an empty cocoa tin, tin snips, wire and Gun Gum to repair the exhaust. Waterproofing the plugs was always a problem and we did many a mile in pouring rain 'firing on three'. I finally covered the engine with a sheet of rubber, made up of cut-open inner tubes. Thereafter, when there was a plug problem, I could stop, whatever the weather, and mop out the wet plug with toilet paper while the engine was still hot enough to dry the plug. In winter I carried a small container of meths and a tin lid. That was to heat the plugs up, out of the engine, when starting was difficult, usually after standing for a week or so in the snow.

Included in the never-to-be-forgotten memories is the time the windscreen shattered. This was on a journey home from Shelf after Christmas. It was raining heavily when it happened on the road from Wakefield to Doncaster. I pushed sufficient glass out so I could see ahead, then stopped. The rain was so heavy that it did not seem a good idea to push the rest of the glass out, so I left it in. I used the plastic sheet off the back window (used to stop it misting up) to cover the hole. We stopped at Uncle Arnold's house in Peterborough for a warm-up and then pressed on to complete the journey in eight hours.

Then there was the time on the way back from Hyeres (near Toulon) when the ignition light came on as we were driving along. Having discovered that I could restore the charge by drawing together the two terminal posts at the top of the dynamo, I held them in position with a bit of string. That saw us safely home and a good few miles beyond that.

I never did manage to beat the 'flat spot', that certain knowledge that enthusiastic pressure on the accelerator was more likely to be met with hesitation rather than a sudden spurt! Yes, my daughter, Rosemary, summed it up saying the Javelin was part of a family affair that lasted for ten years.

E.A. Askew, Bexley, Kent

Channel hop

My father, Roland Hopwood, owned a 1934 Jowett long saloon, which had a mind of its own! It could sense when we were nearing home because it would sail up Box Hill, near Corsham (possibly because it had the prevailing wind behind it!) but only creep up the steepish hill out of Marlborough towards the Savernake Forest. I think the car sensed it was going away from home – we were lucky to do more than 5mph up there. The highest speed that we ever recorded was 53mph going down a hill near Sittingbourne in Kent.

He later went on to buy a Javelin, which was his pride and joy. When I returned from working in Africa in September 1963, my mother and father and younger brother toured France and Germany, meeting up with me in Lausanne in Switzerland. I had got off the ship in Naples and travelled by rail to Lausanne from where we returned straight back to England.

Before I had joined the family, they had taken the Javelin up several alpine passes and the car seemed a bit tired by the time I arrived. When we checked the car we found there was virtually no water in the radiator and precious little brake fluid left.

As I remember it – and my memory may be quite faulty – the Channel hop, from Le Touquet to Lydd, took about twenty minutes in the *Bristol Freighter* and cost about £6 (return) for the car and about 30*s* for each passenger. Passengers sat on slatted wooden benches like an old bus; it was extremely convenient though.

Roger Hopwood, Warminster

Bill Petty's Javelin, registered LHN 990, parked outside their house in 1956 – no garage, but street parking was not a problem in those days. Note the gas streetlight behind the car!

LHN 990

I left school in 1950 and started work in an architect's office. The boss had a 1949 turquoise-blue Javelin. I had seen a couple before, but had never driven in one; it was a magic carpet! At the time the austere years were still with us and other cars were either pre-war, or post-war built to pre-war designs.

After the first drive I was smitten, but it was five years before I was able to buy one. I bought a 1949 turquoise-blue Javelin in 1955, registered LHN 990, which was affectionately known as 'Jess', I sold her in mid-1960 for £200. This was soon after joining the Army for my national service; £1 or thereabouts a week was not enough to run a car on. In 1955 the Javelin was head and shoulders above anything else on the road, and to this day can only be described as a beautiful design. The 1956 Suez Crisis caused petrol rationing but it was surprising how the Javelin could make the most of what there was.

My car was previously owned by a gentleman who was Inspector of Taxi Cabs in Darlington. At some stage the crank had been changed to the oval web type. The oil pressure, or lack of it, was always a problem but never fully resolved. I had new bearings fitted on two occasions while I had the car.

Before spending a week's holiday in Scotland, I had a new tyre fitted at the front of the car (a £3 remould). During the tour I became aware of, and increasingly irritated by, an annoying vibration of which my brother and sister profusely denied being aware. Towards the end of the week I found the cause: the tyre had not been properly seated and the wheel rim was gouging the tyre wall in one spot. I drove to a small garage, the tyre was deflated and properly seated, and driving was bliss once again.

I drove the car in all sorts of weather conditions and snow and ice never seemed to

Mrs June Petty stands proudly with the family Javelin, registered LHN 990.

A nice country view, showing the Petty Javelin, taken in Bilsdale, near Chop Gate. It was probably taken in early 1957, as the car still has its radiator muff on.

Used to be a long journey

It's a big hill; steep, curving. No chance to take a run at it. Lorries block you to a crawl. Throttle. Brakes. Throttle. It takes the guts out of a car. And out of a driver, too.

But not this car; not this driver. A clear patch and you put your foot down in 3rd. In a flash the needle says 50—you're away.

How long have you been travelling now? Two hours? Three hours? Travelling fast—60, 65, 70, 75. But there's no strain. You're fresh; relaxed.

A corner comes and goes; and another and another. A surprising absence of roll. You work out your average. It's high. Somehow this car grips a bend and straightens it out: comes to a hill and flattens it down.

You sit enjoying it.

It's a good road now. But there have been bad patches; they got lost in the torsion bar suspension, and not a kick in the steering. Only your eyes noticed.

Two hours to go. The light fades. You snap on the head lights; brightly reassuring in the dusk.

This used to be a long journey. But this car conquers distance.

And what about space? Plenty. You can take up to six with luggage—and still have driving fun.

This car is a waste of money if you don't care what a car *does*. There's such a lot built into it that doesn't really show until you have it in your hands. Once tried, you'll say 'I'd rather go by Javelin!'

Top speed 78 m.p.h. Acceleration 0-60 in 22.2 secs.
Horizontally opposed flat-four 50 B.H.P. engine.

★ *Javelins came 1st and 3rd in the Monte Carlo Rally, 1½ litre class.*

1½ LITRE JOWETT JAVELIN

 take a good look when it passes you

pose much of a problem, maybe I was just young and foolhardy! I became adept at changing fan belts, I seemed to chew them up at the rate of two a year. Once again they were a relatively cheap item at 2 shillings each. I changed the brake linings front and rear only once in my ownership. In those days you took the brake shoes into a garage and they riveted on new linings while you waited.

Paint on the wheel arches needed attention so, with coarse wet and dry, I cleaned it up on all four arches and brush painted, primered, undercoated and top coated, carefully flatting with wet and dry between the coats. I gradually became more and more enthusiastic and flatted more and more to blend in the brushed areas. Yes, I eventually ended up spraying the whole car! I was not aware at the time, of course, just how thick the metal used was and how solid and well put together the whole car was compared to present-day cars. What would the Javelin be like with upgraded brakes, discs all round, electronic ignition and maybe flatter tyres? I cannot think of anything else really needed for twenty-first century motoring!

I presently run a 1979 Renault 16TL which in many respects reflects the Javelin, with torsion bar suspension and steering column gear change, a flat floor and remarkable space.

Bill Petty, Penrith, Cumbria

Another view of my Javelin, waiting for a steam train to go past at Grosmont railway station. This station is used regularly in the Heartbeat *series.*

Zimbabwe

After service in the forces I went to Zimbabwe (then Southern Rhodesia) to teach in a school there. I was posted to an out of the way village about a hundred miles from Salisbury, the capital. Everybody had a car but they were difficult to come by. I bought a second-hand American Plymouth, one of the few cars available. I ran this for a couple of years, then decided to change it and bought a Jowett Javelin, which was a delight!

I moved to Senoia (now Chenoyi) as superintendent of a boarding hostel and took the Javelin with me. I often came to Salisbury (now Harare) on a Saturday and had the car serviced there, driving back was a joy.

From Senoia I took the family to Zambia, travelling on very bad roads, and had very little trouble. The only fault I had was that the battery was under the seat, and, with some of the roads we travelled on, acid sometimes escaped!

I used this car until I came on leave in 1953 when I took advantage of a special offer by a British company who would take my car in exchange and deliver my new car to Southampton. I was sorry to give up my Javelin, but it was such a good offer.

I returned to England in 1969 and was head of a school in Horden, Co. Durham; I later came to York. I still hear from people I knew in Zimbabwe and regret the conditions there now.

Alan McFarlane, York

PYJ 463 – bought from Benny Lynch

My first car was a Javelin, which was registered PYJ 463, it was gold-coloured with red leather seats. I bought it from Benny Lynch, who you may remember was a boxing champion. I eventually traded it in for a Saab 95 because my wife ran it (the Jowett) into a ditch and twisted the front steering.

The crankshaft broke far away from home, but I managed to get it back home and took the engine out. Whilst it was in my lock-up garage, I got a note from my employer saying that I had been seen speeding on site. I sent a note back saying if he could tell me how a car with no engine could do that, I would be forever grateful!

Whilst I was stripping the engine block down, intending to replace the crankshaft with one from a Jupiter, a 'knowledgeable' succeeded in cracking the crankcase. After a while I got a good replacement engine with a Jupiter crankshaft, and it soldiered on for some years after that.

One of my favourite tricks to mend exhaust pipes was to wrap spring shim round the hole and fix that with circlips. One of my most alarming experiences was to forget to put anti-freeze in. After an unexpected frost, I found the cylinder-block blanking discs on the garage floor. I just popped them in and all was well.

When I used to go back home, up the A9, I used to love doing the '3rd gear' trick. As you probably know, this involved waiting until someone came up from behind and ready to pass. I would get into 3rd gear, wait until he was level, then put my foot down and wave back to him as I disappeared into the distance. I was rather young at the time!

I have often looked for Jowetts at vintage car rallies, but no success. For a long time now I have been a Volvo fan, and have been through three different models. My current one is a well-tuned 440 Turbo diesel. No need for the 3rd gear trick now, I can tell you!

John W. Bruce, Dingwall, Ross-Shire

A nice York-registered Javelin on a caravanning holiday.

KCE 716 – My first proper car

I enjoyed my Javelin, KCE 716, which was the first 'proper' car I owned. Before its advent I ran motorcycles and a BSA three-wheeler.

The Javelin was a pleasant and quite fast car, with the best steering column gear change I have ever used. The car had three faults. It corroded on the rear wings just aft the door – they all did, and it succeeded in breaking its crankshaft (again a well-known fault caused by poor design and an apparent lack of understanding of stress concentration). The replacement crankshafts were better. One I seem to recall was the 'black-sided' shaft, the other, and even better, was a polished and properly blended design.

I was in the RAF at the time the shaft broke and I drove the car some ten miles to the station (very slowly) from the remote wilds of Norfolk. The other, and persistent, problem was sticking of the exhaust valve of number 4? cylinder, the one all the gasses passed. The valve would stick open and then close with a clonk like a big end going home. I remember having the head off with monotonous frequency to clean the stem. I tried various remedies but finally sorted things out by cutting the guide short.

Michael Thurbon, Maidenhead, Berks

WMD 460

In December 1959 I bought a 1951 Javelin from Performance Cars Ltd, a second-hand car outfit based somewhere in North London, for £245; it was registered WMD 460.

I then went on to work for a civil engineering contractor, and together that car and I went all over the country. It took me through some of the most important parts of my life, including meeting my wife-to-be, getting married, and eventually producing two children (my wife and I, not the car!).

To a man's woman

As a woman you're probably not impressed with such triumphs ... winner of International trial and speed events. That's for the enthusiast. But you hope he won't buy a car that's built just for speed — you want comfort too.

Well, here's the Javelin. Different from what you'd imagined — much more roomy. Not super sports but family design.

Sit in the passenger's seat. Deep and plenty of room. Soft, lolling arm-rests. She's an intriguing car!

And in the back you can doze a journey away — so comfortable. Your eye flickers over the rich fittings ... pleased ... taking it all in.

And yet he said this was a high performance car. He talked about acceleration and speeds up to nearly 60 m.p.h. He mentioned the powerful brakes, the torsion bar suspension that cushioned the roughest road, and gripped the corners.

This car is both. His for speed — yours for comfort. Seating up to six — a new form of travel — owning the road she rides.

This car is a waste of money if you don't care what a car does. There's such a lot built into it that doesn't really show until you have it in your hands. Once tried, you'll say 'I'd rather go by Javelin!'

Top speed, electrically timed, 78 m.p.h. Acceleration 0–60 m.p.h. in 22.2 secs. ("*The Motor*" Road Test). Horizontally opposed flat-four 50 B.H.P. engine. Javelin saloon: £595, plus purchase tax £166.0.7. Javelin saloon de luxe: £695, plus purchase tax £193.16.1.

★ There are over 200 fully qualified Service Agents in Great Britain.

1½ LITRE

JAVELIN

take a good look when it passes you

JOWETT CARS LIMITED, Idle, Bradford and 48, Albemarle Street, Piccadilly, W.1

The speedometer jammed at 97,519 on the second time round, and I drove it like that for so many miles that the figure is permanently imprinted on my mind to this day. So I expect it must have done 250,000 miles at least. We sold it some time late in 1962, for two reasons:

i) The body was no longer connected to the chassis, due to rot caused by the then new custom of salting the roads.

ii) The acidic waters of Teesdale, where I lived at the time, were very aggressive to aluminium when hot, and were eating away the engine block. With two young children, I had neither the time nor the money to do the car up. I therefore traded it in to Keighley's of Darlington for a three-year-old Morris Traveller. It was a willing little car, true enough, but it was a sad change from my Javelin!

The Javelin was extremely temperamental and moody. When we were both on the same wavelength it was superb, but when it had one of its off days we all suffered. The gasket on the timing cover went once and blew engine oil all over the engine bay. This was at Nuneaton and was very spectacular at the time!

I did all the usual things to the car, like one fine bank holiday in August 1960 deciding to take out the engine and strip it. In the end I put in a new crankshaft, clutch plate etc., and that seemed to please it.

I always drove at 70mph in all weathers, day and night, and always had 32mph on pool petrol. It went round corners very well and was the most comfortable car I have ever had. I liked everything being adjustable, such as the suspension height and track rod ends etc. I found the small petrol tank a bit of a nuisance as I did so much long-distance night driving, and finding petrol could be a problem. The twin carburettors were a right swine if I got dirty petrol. I did once on a heavily snowing Good Friday night, when I was driving from Preston in Lancashire to Epsom in Surrey. Especially when you bear in mind that there were no motorways then, I was still busy building the very first one, the Preston bypass, now part of the M6. That night I stripped those twin Zenith carbs, with their seven jets each, roughly every twenty-five miles over a 240-mile journey. That was a trip I really did not enjoy!

That car took us all over the country in all weathers and was a good friend to us, with occasional bad days. I once went through a ford near Kenilworth at 5.00 a.m. in September 1959, on my way to Birmingham. This broke one of the cylinder heads, but luckily she still ran and I managed to reach Birmingham on two cylinders. I was able to find a dealer selling Jowett spares and bought a new head. I fitted this the same day and no damage seemed to be done. My Javelin went through snow, ice, mud, over ploughed fields etc. but, after Kenilworth, never through open water!

I had all the usual laughs, like people who thought the engine was at the rear, and people with sports cars who tried to keep up with me but ran out of road (especially Triumph Heralds!). I did find that if I used the semaphore signals at speeds of over 60mph, they had a tendency to snap off, so I just stopped using them.

I think all young car designers should be made to study the Javelin, and give it proper respect, then we would have less of the rubbishy tin box repmobiles that litter our roads now. This is why I drive a Lada; it's the closest thing I can get these days to having any sort of engineering excellence. It is an engineer's car rather than a salesman's tin box. So come back Jowett, even though you were very expensive, and as contrary as a drunk pig, I miss you. All I have left is the old maintenance manual and pleasant memories.

H.C. Devonshire, Darlington, Co. Durham

Gerald Palmer at the wheel of an early Javelin, registered FKU 279, during its Continental trip.

The next two letters are from non-Javelin owners, but they have a common theme; they relate to the prototype Javelin and its designer, Gerald Palmer.

Hitch-hiking

I never owned a Javelin, but ran two Jowett '8's for many years [*detailed in the pre-war section. NS*] but I did have a ride, by accident, in one of the prototype Javelins. During the war I was in the Army, and, for a time, was stationed in Otley. I was visiting some friends in Pateley Bridge and was hitchhiking there. I was in uniform and in those days everybody would stop for a serviceman. I was picked up by a very strange car, which I had never seen the like of before, and I was told by the driver it was a Jowett. I told him we had two at home and was very interested as they were nothing like this car!

He told me it was a new four-cylinder model, which was under test, and would be launched after the war. He said that every day it was driven from the works in Idle into the countryside to test for faults. At this time he said it had done several thousand miles already. He said that on one occasion the bonnet blew open and the car nearly crashed, so they came back and designed a better bonnet catch! When we got to where he dropped me off, he got out of the car and opened the bonnet so I could see the new flat-four engine design and spoke about its smoothness and good performance.

After reading your book *Jowett 1901-1954*, I am sure the person who picked me up was Gerald Palmer, the car's designer!

Leslie Beech, Croxley Green, Herts

Prototype

I thought you might be interested in how I first heard of the Javelin. As a schoolboy in the Brighouse area in the twenties and thirties, I was brought up with Jowetts. My father always said that he couldn't afford a new Jowett, so we never actually owned one.

In 1941 when I was a junior clerk at Martins Bank, Wyke, Bradford, I volunteered for aircrew duties in the RAF. I served in the Middle East with a Wellington Bomber Squadron. I returned home on leave in 1943 and visited my maiden aunt, who was house-keeper to a bachelor living in a flat in Manningham Lane, Bradford. He was in fact, Gerald Palmer, the designer of the Javelin.

I remember being shown a streamlined Jowett with a split screen, which was parked outside the flat. This car was, of course, one of the prototypes which was being tested during the war. It would be launched as the Javelin in 1947, but by that time it had a one-piece curved windscreen.

I hope this will be of interest to you, I am now eighty-one years old and find that my memory is fine for things that happened sixty years ago but, as many people say, I forget what I had for last Sunday's lunch!

Reg G. Thackeray, Altringham, Cheshire

[*Reg first wrote to me in 1991. At the time I was amazed that a prototype car would have been openly used so long before its launch. I wrote to Gerald Palmer, who remembered living in Manningham Lane during the war. He said he would have parked the car outside the flat at times. He also drove an early production model, registered FKU 279, on the Continent on holidays in 1948 and 1949. Sadly Gerald died in June 1999 so I cannot ask him to confirm if he remembered picking up a hitch-hiker in the car also! NS*]

The early Javelin, registered FKU 279, being off-loaded from the ferry at the start of a Continental holiday and test run. The driver is Gerald Palmer, the car's designer.

Racing model

I owned a Javelin during the 1960s, it was a late series 3 model so had the strengthened crankshaft, but I still managed to break it! Admittedly, that was after I had seen off an annoying man in a 2.4 Jaguar who wanted to race, so I suppose it was my own fault. Like most owners, I had never previously experienced the combination of space, performance, comfort and economy, which the Javelin offered. It was certainly the best car of its time and its demise was a tragedy. It had its own little foibles, which only made the car more endearing!

Icing of the carburettors was a regular occurrence in cold weather; I would get two or three miles on my way to work, when it would stop. I would have no option but to wait until it had thawed out. After that, I could continue on with no further trouble. The other quirk was that the spark plugs sat in small recesses, which would fill with water when I drove through a puddle, causing another short stop.

Once or twice, the centre bearing on the propshaft came loose, causing a dreadful vibration. It was quite embarrassing having to get underneath and fix it if you were wearing decent clothes. Against that, the pleasure of cruising along the few motorways we had at around 80mph was only rivalled by cars with much bigger engines.

I believe that the restoring of the sealing of the crankcase after major engine work was difficult – certainly the garage that replaced my crankshaft never achieved it. I eventually swapped the Javelin for a Mk VII Jaguar, which was not a wise move, as it turned out.

Freddy Evans, Woodbury Salterton, Exeter

Pride and joy

I owned a Javelin in the 1960s, it was a battleship grey, but I cannot remember what the colour was called [*Athena Grey. NS*] The seats were a deep rich-maroon leather, the armrests were lowered by solid chrome-plated struts that were the envy of all my friends!

The person who sold me the car was called Mr Barton of Hastings. He had recently returned from India and had taken over a small petrol station in St Leonards. I do not know if the car came with the business or not, as there were two or three cars that were described as 'old bangers' hidden away in the lower depths of the building when he bought the business. I would guess it was, as I do not think he brought it with him.

Two days after I bought the car I took it on a local rally, and realised just how fast the car was. I was going down a long straight outside Bexhill, when I was doing 80mph. I would have been hard-pushed to get my previous car, a pre-war Morris 8, up to 35mph!

This car was my pride and joy and I will have run it for between two and three years. The car started to burn a lot of oil, and I was having to fill up with oil every time I put petrol in! There was so much blue smoke, it was like a battleship going past. Finally I suffered a broken crank but was able to buy a replacement from a Jowett specialist at Bexley Heath. When this was fitted and the engine was rebuilt, it ran much better.

My friend, who worked at the garage where I bought the car from, borrowed it from time to time. On one occasion a new Vauxhall ran into the back of the Javelin and the driver was concerned at what damage would have been done to the car. The Vauxhall's front end was badly damaged and the fan had been pushed through the radiator. After checking over the Javelin, the only damage to it was a cracked reflector glass!

There must have been a short circuit behind the dashboard, as I had a major panic when a fire broke out. I instinctively pushed my hand up behind the dash, and was lucky as it did not spread, but I had a nasty burn on my hand. I did my best to repair the wires with insulation tape, but this was only a limited success. The car continued to run well for a time, but then disaster struck! My father had taken the car on this occasion and parked it outside, where he was working. Later he was told a car was on fire outside – yes, it was the Javelin! I think one of the wires must have shorted again, and, while the car was parked, the car had caught fire and was burnt-out.

When I first saw the car, I was shocked as I had never seen a fire-damaged car before and it looked a real mess. I was broken-hearted; needless to say the car was a write-off. My dad came to my assistance and passed on his Ford Consul to me, so my Jowett days were over.

This was the most memorable car I have ever owned; I loved the sound it made, the speed and the comfort.

Len Cooper, Hastings

Jowett Reminiscences

In 1968, while I was 'between cars', I was offered (for £17) a 1951 Jowett Javelin, NKP 355, mileometer reading 86,222, that had been taken to a scrap yard, but which the yard thought 'too good to scrap'. The bodyshell was in pretty good condition – the chassis had had new bottoms welded to the two main members, and the body had been resprayed in a very dark green. Only a crack behind a rear door, with a white plastery face, betrayed the car might not be all metal. Inside, the car had bench seats with leather upholstery.

The engine (reconditioned engine RO 14392, an oily piece of paper tells me) was rather another matter, however, as it only had three compressions, and only had oil pressure for about the first 200yds. Also, as bought, the choke cable was missing, which made starting a bit problematic – but my mother said she could always tell whether I had been able to get away (the car was parked round a corner) by whether there was a blue haze hanging in the air all the way down the road. Later, I got a choke cable from another Javelin in the same scrap yard, and also made a hand throttle out of Meccano and string.

I was told you needed to prime the carburettors before starting, with a few pulls of the priming lever on the petrol pump. So, to avoid having to open the bonnet every morning, I secured a leather shoelace through the hole in the priming lever, and led it upwards and out between two slats of the grille, ending in a ring. This must have stopped it from slipping back in, through the grille, so that all I had to do was pull on the ring to prime the carburettors. This worked well (in conjunction with fitting a proper choke cable), except that I found that the car still started even when I forget to do it – having made it easy, I found it wasn't necessary after all! Even so, starting was always chancy.

The car did twenty-five miles to the gallon, and twenty-five miles to the pint. A journey to Bournemouth and back (210 miles) used a gallon of oil (or thereabouts, as it was very difficult to see the level of the brand-new oil on the dipstick!).

One time, the boy next door pulled up alongside me on his motorbike at the Iron Bridge, Southall, traffic lights, and nodded to me, so we both took off smartly when the lights changed, and the traffic behind completely disappeared! We never saw them again! They must all have been too busy shutting their windows and vents and turning their fans off as quickly as they could!

Another neighbour who had to follow me sometimes said the car was 'absolutely foul to drive behind'. The crankshaft was also rather worn, so that the engine clonked

The 1951 Javelin, registered NKP 355, bought by David Bowater in 1968 for £17. These pictures were taken on 19 January 1969.

noticeably up to about 50mph in top, where obviously the crankshaft did not get all the way across to one side before being pushed back towards the other, so it all smoothed out. However, with the engine stationary, I did once try pulling up and down on the crankshaft pulley, and could see the fan belt going in and out. The further information on the oily piece of paper, 'Main bearing size STD, Big end size STD, Rear thrust, Bore size .005' was definitely a case of 'Once upon a time'.

Mentioning the petrol pump reminds me that one morning the engine only gave a couple of coughs, and I found that the glass 'bowl' of the petrol filter was broken – with no sign of damage or vandalism to the car – but just a road chipping lying alongside the bowl. I could only imagine that, the previous day, the chipping had come through the grille and cracked the bowl, but that the bowl had not actually fallen apart until the engine cooled down in the evening. A bit of a mystery even so!

I changed the spark plugs soon after getting the car – due to the flat-four layout, of course, they are just inboard of the front wheels. However, by turning the wheels on full left lock, I was able to reach the left two, and vice versa. Fortunately it wasn't until later that I read that you had to take the wheels off to do this! This manoeuvre was also useful for soaking up the water with paper tissues after rain.

Once, at the traffic lights just outside Hanger Lane Station, the engine died just as I was turning right, and I instantly diagnosed ignition failure, due to the sudden cessation. It only took another moment to see that, instead of cancelling the trafficator, I had turned the engine off.

In August 1968 I bought a much newer car, a 1964 Singer Vogue III Automatic, but I was disappointed to find that thirteen years' progress didn't seem to count for much in performance, or fuel consumption, or handling, all of which were worse in the Singer than in the Jowett!

I advertised the Jowett for sale for £50 (it would have been worth £300 if it had had £300 spent on it), but got no response. So, on 8 March 1969, I took the car to Weston Turville (mileometer reading 89,232), and gave it to the then secretary of the Jowett Club, Mr A.N. Wright – he accepted the car as a gift, but gave me 30s for a flasher set I had bought but not fitted (except, I think, for the switch, which must have worked rather like the ignition switch!).

David Bowater, Acton, London

[I received a second letter from David, which follows. NS]

While working for the London Borough of Hounslow in 1968, when I was using my Jowett, I heard a story from Mr Bill Hardcastle, a colleague there, middle-aged at the time, that may be known in Jowett circles anyway, but I will repeat it as far as I remember it. A young apprentice was working on the engine assembly line, in the 1920s or '30s, I expect putting the spark plugs in, but he dropped (I think) one of the little washers that go on with the plug lead, through the hole and into the cylinder. He could have said nothing – but he owned up. Benjamin Jowett not only did not tell him off for dropping the washer in, but gave him sixpence for owning up, saying that if he had said nothing, no-one would have known, but the engine could have been badly damaged. This reaction was thought to be typical of Ben Jowett's kindly attitude.

Another colleague at Hounslow, Frank Keal, told me about a Javelin he once owned. This story was that he was driving up an upgrade, and for whatever reason – probably including traffic conditions – he stayed

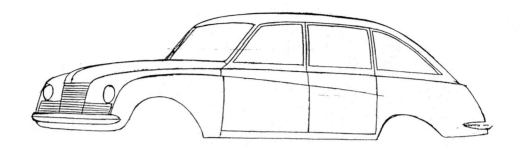

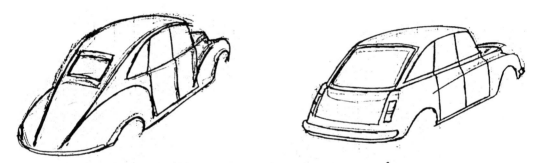

The suggested future designs of the Javelin by David Bowater.

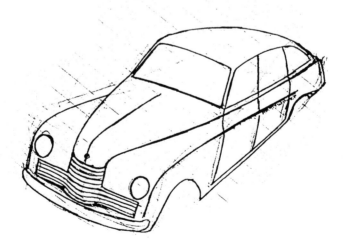

in third gear for some miles, and the result was that the third gear bearings ran. He attributed this to the smaller sump of the flat-four engine (compared to an in-line engine) giving less cooling, so making the engine oil hotter, which helped overheat the gearbox.

He also said that at one period he noticed that small items, like pairs of gloves, would appear in, or disappear from, the car. He eventually found that, at the pub that he went to at lunchtimes, another man with an identical Javelin also visited, and either set of keys would fit either car! (But, bearing in mind we have heard this sort of story about Fords, I daresay it is more a case of 'My car body was built by Briggs' than 'My car was a Jowett!')

Seeing a postcard of the Zig Zag Road (I think it is) at Box Hill, reminded me that it was on climbing the sharpest corner there that I became confused about the steering column gear lever. I changed up instead of down; I had my mother and two aunts in the car, and mother protested about the crunching of gears and the lack of smooth forward motion!

Still, I was not the only one to get confused – I was with a friend in his Ford Consul Mark II when he was teaching his wife to drive, and she pulled away from a (flat) cross-roads on the A4 or somewhere, gently feeding in the clutch, and feeding it in, and feeding it in … until she got to about 30mph … by which time it became apparent that she was in top gear, and always had been. Good clutch control, though!

My car had a curious feature, namely a cable coming up from the front middle of the front floor somewhere and ending in either one, or two, bare wires. When these were joined or earthed (I can't remember which), there was a clonk from underneath. I never did find out what this was.

David Bowater, Acton, London

Rebuilding the engine

I had a 1952 model Javelin and ran it for six or seven years. I acquired it in 1962 with the engine requiring attention. The cars were reputed to have gasket, starter and gearbox problems. I was fairly keen to run the car, but was chiefly interested in having a go at its troubles, so the engine state was as hoped for.

The oval web crank was needing a regrind and was already about -060in. I found a flat web in fair nick. These were reputed to break. I have a hefty-ish right foot, so we'd soon establish whether this was true or not. I made divots to go in the ready-drilled holes in the hope of improving the balance and, therefore, the durability. It broke. The cause of the gasket trouble was pretty obvious. The liners were supposed to be proud of the block, I believe 012in. The optimists had specified a halite-type gasket for the liner to pull down on. Surprise, surprise; the liners kept sinking. Easily rectified by fitting annealed copper seals coated with Welseal. The original gaskets were copper-asbestos-copper. I had found a helpful Javelin man who kept spares. He had improved gaskets consisting of copper-asbestos-steel. With this setup I never blew a gasket. I did get a bit too clever later and suffered for it.

The starter problem was equally obvious: the ring gear was shoved on from the wrong end. Presumably it had been designed for [a] pre-engage starter then produced with inertia engagement. I had the same trouble the other way round with my Triumph. Simply drill and tap six equi-distance two BA holes half in flywheel and half in ring, screw set bolts in and cut them off flush. I very much liked the close-ratio box. Unfortunately, I continually broke the first gear with this arrangement. I could have soft-pedalled first gear but I'm not partial to cripple's motoring, if you know what I mean. The rather agricultural wide-ratio setup, which obviously put even more load on first gear, lasted forever. Close ratio being the later arrangement, it can be assumed the material spec was lowered to save money. Typical for what passes for engineering in those days and in the present.

I used Jupiter pistons and carbs. It would smooth out completely and go up to an indicated 94mph before I chickened out. Trying the Jupiter exhaust slightly improved torque but lost about 7mph top end. I also made up a four-pipe system of equal length. This got rid of that nasty throb but I had forgotten that the ports exited at a fairly sharp angle. I lobbed it (the exhaust, not the car). There had been a slight water leak under the right bank. Naturally one would think this was just a question of tightening up a hose clip. I always was a bloody optimist. As we were going away in the car for a holiday, I got down there with a screwdriver. Lo and behold, there was a very convincing crack from front to rear of the water jacket. As I said, I had been just that little bit too clever and unthinking. The last time I had built the engine I had fitted even more super gaskets: steel, asbestos and steel. Nobody was going to blow one of those. The unequal expansion of the ally block and the steel liners needed a tiny bit of flexibility and it wasn't getting it with this almost solid gasket, so it took matters into its own hands and introduced a bit of give in the water jacket. The language was not nice but I did have a spare block and fitted it in less than three days.

I fitted a thermometer in the sump. At the time I was employed by Vauxhall's in the Experimental Engine Test Department. I forget the figure now but there was a limit to the oil temperature the operator was allowed to use. Top and bottom. I could not afford the proper Javelin cooler but I had fitted a length of that furry-type copper tube as used on various auto transmissions. This helped; nevertheless I was quite surprised how near the magic top figure I attained hurrying down the M1 to London, also how little it dropped creeping through London. Of course a flat-four heats the oil from both sides and is only cooled from the bottom. An in-line job cools it from both sides and the bottom. We did a lot of miles fairly quickly in the car. The handling was acceptable in standard trim but was improved when using Michelin X tyres, the only radials obtainable at that time. Because they were a quarter of an inch wider than the normal tyres, it was necessary to deflate the spare to get it into the carrier.

I did not like the bench seat. My car was a deluxe model with leather upholstery and a meaty armrest. Not as good as the old Riley's bucket seats, but better than a kick up the rough end, if you know what I mean. The youngest oaf was prone to settle on this while awake. The car was a bit on the noisy side but it never let us down. Even when the crank broke on the way back to work after lunch; hurrying along the motorway, the oil pressure dropped and a tinny noise developed. I coaxed it back to work and nursed it home through the urban jungle. In spite of the fumble-footed driving, the car never had to be towed home. Road roar was very noticeable after the Riley with its hefty chassis; that car made up for it with wind noise, as it had no door seals.

One other adventure I had was with flat-top pistons I got made. I was told these used A60 forgings. I could not imagine forging ally but there you go. One not very fine afternoon going home from work through the urban jungle, I suddenly noticed a smokescreen forming behind me. Where I had come from was completely invisible; one of those flat-tops had grown a hole. Like the Jupiter exhaust, this experiment gained torque and I lost the top end. I went back to the Jupiter pistons and lived happily ever after.

My previous Javelin, registered GJF 664, pictured at Grosmont railway station, with Sir Nigel Gresley *on 29 September 1996. I sold this car when I bought my present Javelin, registered FFR 900.*

Another shot of my old Javelin GJF 664, which was pictured at a small garage between Scarborough and Whitby. Sadly, the garage was sold earlier this year, and the old petrol pumps have now been removed.

gay deceiver

You've heard incredible stories about this car—stories of International race triumphs; unbelievably high average speeds. And frankly you're doubtful.

Now as you inspect her close up, you still think it can't be. She looks so comfortable, even sedate . . . so harmless somehow. Can that neat, tapering bonnet house such formidable power?

Then you settle down in the deep driving seat and touch the controls . . . and after a while you know this Javelin's been smiling at you all the time because those cars ahead seem almost stationary; and as you glide silently up behind, you realize you're travelling fast—very fast. And you brake . . .

Quickly the needle slips back to 40— yes, you were up in the 70's and the whole car was smooth and steady. You didn't even notice. The torsion bar suspension holds you gently to the corners, the road seems velvet smooth, the short neat bonnet lets you see and relax at the same time and the precision steering is just that. It's all so easy in this Javelin.

Now you know it. This car, so disarmingly innocent—so spacious—has all the speed of victory in her veins.

This car is a waste of money if you don't care what a car does. There's such a lot built into it that doesn't really show until you have it in your hands. Once tried, you'll say, 'I'd rather go by Javelin!'

Top speed, electrically timed. 78 m.p.h. Acceleration 0-60 m.p.h. in 22.2 secs. —(*The Motor* Road Test.) Horizontally opposed flat-four 50 B.H.P. engine.

Javelin Saloon: £595
    plus purchase tax £166.0.7.
Javelin Saloon de luxe: £695
    plus purchase tax £193.16.1

There are over 200 fully qualified Service Agents in Great Britain

See the Javelin at Stand 162 at the International Motor Exhibition, Earls Court.

1½ LITRE

JAVELIN

take a good look when it passes you

Although this was the best column change four-speed setup there ever was, my wife refused to drive it all the while we had ran it. When we acquired a Mk 9 Jaguar she did condescend to bring the Javelin home. She had refused to drive the Riley with its pre-selector box. We ran a Standard 10 for her amusement. Funny things, women.

We did the Lake District among other things, including a restart on Hardnot Pass. No problem apart from slight wheelspin on a dry road. I think this was the longest journey we did. Up the right-hand side to Whatsit-on-Tees and down the left-hand side from Windermere. With a camping trailer. Only troubles were an oiled plug when we were almost at the Lakes after creeping across – we had camped for the night at a funny-named place. You do have 'em up there. We did have to buy a new tyre for the trailer. Limited to 50mph we were passed by all and sundry, and a kindly gentleperson indicated to us that there was summat amiss wi't' trailer. The tyre was nearly on fire, and well past repair, which was a real pity as there was plenty of mileage in the thing and they don't grow on trees. One could go on as they say, but I'll give it a miss from here on, but I never did sort the main rear problem.

M.C.D. Witts, Luton, Beds

GBK 121

I owned a 1952 Javelin, which was registered GBK 121, for several years; it was a two-tone car, fawn-coloured on the top and black below. I travelled with the family to every country this side of the Iron Curtain in her. On one occasion we took the car to Imperia on the Italian Riviera, staying in a campsite. It was of great interest to the German visitors, who wondered at the shape of the car, the engine layout and the thickness of the coachwork.

At the time I was living in Burgess Hill in West Sussex and there were two other Javelin enthusiasts I knew of in the area. One of them was a mechanical engineer, the other was a marine engineer. Together we discovered a Javelin, which had half sunk in the Lewes floods, and bought it for £25. Thus we had between the three of us an extra engine we could do up and interchange from time to time.

The only faults that I can remember was that it overheated on the long Swiss Mountain passes, so I always carried extra water. Also, as you will know, in heavy rain and wet conditions, water would splash up into the plug holders in the heads, just next to the front wheels. I always carried a block of blotting paper (pinched from work); this always sufficed in drying them out.

Now at the age of eighty-seven, I still reminisce about the leather bench seats, front and back, the steering column gear change and twin carburettors. Also the below-body driveshaft which always took some balancing after an engine change!

How I looked after that car, the best one I have ever had. It was so well polished, I could have shaved by looking into the coachwork! I have had many cars since and only wish I had kept the Javelin instead of selling it for £45 in 1974!

Tom Hammond, Uxbridge, Middlesex

KOF 757 and DST253

The first Javelin I owned was a light green one, which I bought for £175 from my brother, Alan; sadly he died two years ago. This was back in 1961, when I was very young. The car was registered KOF 757, and I was very proud of it. It was a superb car, and was a great improvement on my first car, which was a pre-war Morris Ten with large running boards.

Unfortunately this car was written off by a Plymouth sedan that the driver lost control of, and hit me broadsides. The Javelin's strength stood up well in the impact, and both drivers survived – hence one of them is writing to you now! I managed to break the plastic steering wheel with my head, which I needed a few stitches for. Sadly that was the end of that beautiful motor, and I just had to have another!

I bought my new Javelin on 17 February 1962, it was registered DST 253 and was coloured black and white. My insurance cost me £1.50, which was a good deal I negotiated with Witley Motors of Oxford. At the time I obtained a pamphlet telling me about the Jowett Car Club, but I never got round to joining. I later swapped the car for a Wolseley 6/90 automatic which I bought in 1963, so the ownership of this car was short and sweet.

The Javelins were well ahead of their time, and with a bit of updating I am sure they would still sell well today. I particularly remember the flat-four engine and the handle under the front bench seat for movement in aft and height. Also the picnic shelf which fitted into the back of the front bench seat into two sockets, so easy and simple, but very practical.

Clive Pether, Paignton, Devon

Touring France

I was a Javelin owner for several years during the 1950s. I bought my first Javelin from Nicholson Motors Ltd of Weymouth; it was a second-hand 1949 model with the one-piece chrome grille. I later bought a 1953 model which had the two-piece aluminium grille. Whilst owning this car I was insrumental in setting up the South West section of the Jowett Car Club. I was an active member of the club until I sold this car, when I moved house in 1968. I spent many happy hours with our Javelins and toured France in one in 1964, right down as far as the Côte d'Azure, with our tents and three young daughters.

Many hours were spent stripping and maintaining engines etc., as I did all my own work in those days – I still have my copy of the maintenance manual. I would love to drive one again to see how it compares with my 1988 Honda Accord.

I am now eighty years of age and still remember my Javelins.

Maurice Wade, Weymouth, Dorset

Javelins 1951, 1952, 1953 and Bob Foster

FAK 798 was a privately-owned Mk 1 Javelin, owned by my father. In 1952 a semi-works Mk 2 EPR 999 was acquired for my father's brother-in-law, George Holdsworth, and my father to enter the Monte Carlo and RAC Rallies. For 1953 EPR 999 was retained for a further season, including another Monte Carlo. The Monte Carlo results were not headline-making but the 1952 RAC Rally did produce high drama. At the end of the rally the results were published showing my father and George Holdsworth as the outright winners in the Javelin. The result was changed the next day after the celebrations following a protest from the eventual winner. Apparently, after allowing only three cars through, one of the special stages became blocked by a crashed car and the whole of the rest of the field were delayed and therefore lost time unfairly. Bob and George were one of the three cars safely through but the organisers cancelled the special stage altogether after the protest and this gave victory to another entry.

In the years concerned, the Javelin was up against Jaguars, Citroens, Lancias and Sunbeam Talbots. The car therefore was at a

LONG, LONG TRAIL·

Photo: Court Photos

World-famous motor-cyclist, Bob Foster, who runs businesses in Parkstone and Blandford, started yesterday from Munich on the first leg of the Monte Carlo rally in his Jowett Javelin. He is one of nearly 40 drivers using Wyresoles—"the steelclaw tread which grips the road." Local concessionaires are Cox & Co., who recently moved their Tyresoles branch to Glyn-road, Upper Parkstone.

Bournemouth men in Monte Carlo final

BOTH Bournemouth entrants in the Monte Carlo Rally are among the eleven British teams who have qualified to take part in to-morrow's regularity tests which will decide the final award winners.

Well-known Parkstone motor cyclist, Bob Foster, who was a Munich starter in his Jowett Javelin, and Bournemouth garage proprietor, George Hartwell (Sunbeam-Talbot), will be competing against the other 50 drivers who have qualified.

"SAFE," WIRE TO WIFE

Both the local men lost points on the gruelling 2,000-mile run, but were placed among nine British teams to take part in the final tests.

Foster's wife learned of her husband's safe arrival in a telegram which arrived at their Parkstone home to-day.

It read: "Arrived—20 minutes late; damaged car front with lorry, but all is well . . ."

Two British drivers completed the gruelling course without loss of marks. They were Stirling Moss, 22-year-old motor racing ace, driving in his first rally, and motor manufacturer, Sidney Allard, veteran rally expert.

FOSTER IN AGAIN

A good deal of interest centres on the entry of Mr. A. R. (Bob) Foster, the former Cheltenham world champion road racing motor-cyclist, now of Parkstone. Going over to four-wheels, he has become famous as a rally driver in little over 12 months, and he was one of the most highly-placed British drivers in the recent "Monte Carlo." His entry is the Jowett he drove in that rally, also in the closed under-2,500 c.c. class.

F. Preece, of 101, Cheltenham-road, Evesham, has entered a Jaguar in the open-car class; and Miss J. M. L. Slatter, 101, Victoria-road, Cirencester, F. J. Merritt, High Garth, Minchinhampton, and E. D. Barnfield, 1, Southern-avenue, Tuffley, are local competitors who have each entered Sunbeam-Talbots in the under-2,500 c.c. closed-car class.

Bob Foster in the 1952 Monte Carlo Rally in his Javelin, registered EPR 999, driving through snow in Col de Braus.

considerable power disadvantage through-out. I believe that a gearbox had to be changed on one of the British Rallies and EPR 999 hit a lorry on the road between stages in the 1952 Monte. Apart from that I believe that the car was reliable during three years of hard competition and I know that the Fosters were all Jowett enthusiasts at the time.

I have no particulars, but as a small boy I remember that talks between my father and Jowetts took place in 1953 regarding an entry of a Jupiter in that year's Le Mans twenty-four-hour race. I regret that nothing ever came of the talks.

You may also be interested to know that around the same period we owned a Bradford van, and this was used in our motorcycle business for delivering and fetch-ing spare parts.

Ian Foster, Wimborne, Dorset

Fearless Foster

At some time in the 1930s a neighbour owned a Jowett and often took us out in it, a great treat for children then, as few people owned cars. Cars all sounded different in those days, you could tell a Morris from a Humber without turning your head and Jowetts were very distinctive – years later I read that they went 'titten fritten'. Exactly.

I worked for Bob Foster in Poole in the early 1950s; Bob won the Lightweight TT in 1936, on his honeymoon, and the Junior TT in 1947. He was World Champion in 1950, rode some fast and fearsome machines and was known as 'Fearless Foster'; he had a prosperous motorcycle business in Poole.

He drove a Jowett Javelin in the Monte Carlo Rally and kept his Javelin for several years. One morning he intended to drive up to Birmingham and Coventry to the huge and prosperous BSA and Triumph factories, and in his usual tearing hurry he called, 'Alan, check my oil!' I was unfamiliar with car engines and gazed at the flat-four without identifying the oil filler. The air intake was prominent and I poured a pint of XXL down it before realising my mistake. 'Either it will 'hydraulic' and bend all the con rods or it will clear; I've got to be off!' cried Bob, and rushed off. It was quite dark in Ashley Road for several minutes after he had gone, and, 'It smoked all the way to Birmingham,' said Bob later. He was not amused when George Savage, a BSA executive, said innocently as he saw him from the factory, 'I didn't know that these were a two-stroke.' I was never allowed to live this down and was known as 'oily Brod' ever after. Yet Bob lent me the car on many occasions and I did my courting in it. Foster was a lovely man and 'a real Englishman'.

We were still using a Bradford van at our Preston shop in 1965. We have always been BMW agents and I never ride anything else. 'Flat twins forever!'

Alan Brodrick, Leyland, Lancaster

ECS 51

My Javelin was registered ECS 51 and I owned it for four years from 1957 to 1961, it was a de luxe 1951 example. I bought it from a used car market in Glasgow in August 1957, shortly after returning from the Far East. I sold the car at the same market in Glasgow. There is not much more I can tell you about the car, except that it was very reliable and enjoyable to drive.

William Crane, Kinross

ADJ 616

I did run a 1949 Javelin for about seven and a half years and then a 1952 model for two and a half years. For a short time I also had a Jupiter, perhaps for a year or so, but I only used it for maybe a thousand miles at the most.

I bought the 1949 Javelin in August 1957 from a garage in Knutsford, Cheshire. It was

The Javelin, registration ECS 51, owned by William Crane from 1957 to 1961. The car was bought at a used car market in Glasgow. The picture was taken on holiday at Lendalfoot in Ayrshire.

She's a Lady

Sometimes you just don't want to use all the zip this car's got. Today you're feeling lazy.

Of course you could whip through the gears and jump to 60 in 22½ seconds and stream along the straight at well over 75, and you could . . .

But today it's different—you feel like crawling . . .

You light a cigarette and drift silently along. Yes, you notice things about this car—how the curved windscreen lets in so much more of the landscape—how practically the bonnet tapers away to give you a close-up view of the road. And the back seat passengers enjoy wide visibility and relax in complete comfort.

Your seat comfy ? Want to be nearer the wheel ? There's no need to stop. Just wind the handle and take the seat forward a bit. That's better. Forward a bit more. That's perfect. You relax and admire the way she takes the curves—the disdainful way she treats the hills.

This is the time to find out the gentle ways of this car. The slightest tiptoe for the clutch and brakes. And that 50 B.H.P. engine just waits for you to tell it what to do—and it does it.

Try and see from how slowly she'll pick up on top gear. That's a test for a 1½ litre car. She does it smoothly from a mere traffic crawl.

A big car flashes past. A whim seizes you. A touch on the throttle and—still in top—you could be . . .

But no. Today you are in the mood to enjoy the Javelin's other qualities — calm and quiet and instantly responsive. Yes—this car's a lady.

This car is a waste of money if you don't care what a car *does*. There's such a lot built into it that doesn't really show until you have it in your hands. Once tried, you'll say ' I'd rather go by Javelin! '

Top speed 78 m.p.h. Acceleration, 0-60 m.p.h. in 22.2 secs. Horizontally opposed flat-four 50 B.H.P. engine.

Javelin saloon : £595 plus P.T. £166.0.7
Javelin saloon de luxe : £695 plus P.T. £193.16.1

1½ LITRE JOWETT JAVELIN

take a good look when it passes you

ix

green and its registration number was ADJ 616. This was my first post-war car and proved to be a most useful acquisition. I was looking for an Austin Devon at the time, but could not afford the ones on offer. The backseat ride decided us on an ex-reps car with a very high mileage. It had a much more unconventional design than I had expected. It was not always trouble-free, but it always got me home (including seventy-five miles with a broken piston) and was very reliable over the seven years that I ran it.

Suspension and bodywork received serious attention over a period of about twelve months when we were not able to afford to run the car. The car was overloaded often, rallied, and frequently driven fast for protracted runs and, although it sounded a little rough, it continued to run. The engine thrived on high revs but was a little short on low-down torque.

I later bought a 1952 example for spares but found it was generally in better condition than my existing one, so I ran this car for two and a half years and used my existing car for spares. During the seven and a half years that the 1949 example gave me service it had two engine strip-downs. The first was for rings and shells and general head polish. The second was to fit new pistons after one had failed. The gearbox also failed twice, early on with broken thrust washers, but it gave no trouble after that.

After driving the 1952 model for a while I had to strip the engine to fit new rings, but after a couple of years one cylinder started burning oil. I fitted the 1949 engine that I had stripped from the old car when I cut it up for spares. This engine still performed faultlessly and improved the car's performance. I used the Javelins when we started camping, mostly in Scotland; they could carry unbelievable amounts of equipment, but still performed well.

I was given a 1952 Jupiter by an associate at work, it was a very interesting sports car, but never very reliable, and rather more trouble than I had time to correct adequately. It was run for about three months, at the time I was running the 1952 Javelin. It was sold to a chap who had helped me with spares, I only ever received a token deposit and never the balance of £10 agreed. He also got most of my Jowett spares; the car was attractive but was a disappointment and rarely used.

My brother also ran similar vehicles over the same period. Both of us had four children and I had my father living with me, so space became the reason for change. We both went to Austin 1800s. We both camped and therefore found the design of the Javelin ideal for carrying all our gear. I also used the 1949 one for a number of overnight local club rallies; normally finishing about halfway down the list. Many eyebrows were raised when such an old vehicle kept up and finished. My entries ended when we had to compete against semi-professionals with support cars and for a time I marshalled. I did win a prize at the JCC Wirral Rally of 1964.

It's almost thirty-five years exactly since I sold my last Javelin but I still have some fond memories of my Jowett days.

Jim Harrison, Burtonwood, Warrington

HWW 415

Our Javelin was jointly owned by my father and I from 1958 to 1961, and was registered HWW 415. I got married in 1961 and left home, soon after this my father sold the car.

The car was originally turquoise blue, but on one of our trips to Scarborough, on the outskirts of Stamford Bridge, and with my father driving, he had to swerve to avoid hitting a little lad who had run across the road. We rolled over and ended upside down in a ditch; the car was badly damaged. We occupants, five of us, which included my

The Javelin of Dennis Noon, registered HWW 415. The car was owned jointly by him and his father from 1958 to 1961. It was originally turquoise blue.

then girlfriend Gwen, fortunately escaped without serious injury. (We have now been married forty-one years.)

The car was towed home some days later, repaired, but the cost of the respraying was somehow left to us, I never did find out why. Anyway we asked for quotations from several places, but were dismayed at the prices they were asking. So we got sheets of wet and dry, bought some black lacquer and good quality camel hair brushes. Yes! You won't believe it; we painted the car by hand. We then spent hours and hours of rubbing and polishing with Brasso. This method was widely used around that date, which would have been about 1960.

It will be about three years ago that a friend of mine tried to trace the car (he is in the police force). Sadly, he told me the car was not licensed or registered, so I can only surmise that it has gone to the happy scrap yard in the sky!

Dennis Noon, Yeadon, Leeds

GCO 189

My husband, Bill Williams, carried on the motor business in Plymouth after the death of his father, Walter Williams, and Uncle Alfred Williams. Sadly my husband died thirty-five years ago now, and the business closed down at that time.

I travelled down to the Jowett works on many occasions to collect new Javelins and Jupiters to drive back to the agency in Plymouth, so I have a lot of happy memo-

The Noon Javelin after the accident that Dennis and his father had in it. The car is pictured outside their house in 1960, after they had painted it black, by hand.

ries of both these models. The first Jowett that I actually owned was a pre-war twin-cylinder sports model with dickey seat, this car was a great joy. The last Jowett Bill and I ran was a Jupiter.

One of the Javelins we owned was registered GCO 189, and I used this car in the London to Penzance Rally. The rally was overseen by the RAC, and set off from Hyde Park Corner, my navigator was Joyce Beaton (now deceased). We left London using the Great West Road, I recall one of the stops was at Blandford. Joyce was an excellent navigator, so all I had to do was drive. You will appreciate that this was over fifty years ago, and I have not been asked to recall it very often! We had driving and manoeuvring tests at the Hoe at Plymouth, which was the one

part of the rally which I well and truly failed!

The Jupiters were of course part of the business; we had several, including a beautiful white one. We used them personally and as demonstrators, so we did not keep them long. After such a long time, I am not sure if I can tell you any more, as I am now rather advanced in years, I am now ninety-four years of age.

Dorothy Williams, Yelverton, Devon

[*Sadly, Dorothy died earlier this year. I would like to send my condolences to her family. NS*]

My loveable moneyhole...

I thought that perhaps you would like to hear about my loveable moneyhole...

As a lad of about nineteen or twenty I saw a silver-coloured Javelin in a used car lot in Gloucester, I think it was a 1953 model priced at £75. This would have been in about 1961 or 1962; it had no MOT, but this was rectified by the garage. I arranged tax and insurance and drove it away, only to run out of petrol after about a mile.

This was the best and most expensive car that I had ever owned so far, a workmate also had one so I knew they 'went well'. The headlights on mine were different to his model; they were the same as those fitted to some Jaguars at the time [*Yes, they were also fitted to the Jupiter. NS*]. I must say that at this time I knew nothing about the mechanics of cars.

My car was comfortable and fast, I was able to get 90mph on the clock, on normal driving at speeds of up to 60mph I got about 30mpg. With the flat-floor and bench seats along with the streamlined looks, it was ideal for a lad of my age. The first thing to go wrong with the car was a rusted-through main brake-pipe. As the car was out of production, the local garage was not able to find one. We had to use one off a Morris Traveller, cut, spliced and silver-soldered to fit by the men in the engineering works where my father worked.

Next on the list was the gearbox reverse gear being unobtainable. This caused a few 'interesting times', so I had to go and see the garage repairman again. He took the gearbox out, but was unable to repair it. I found an address in *Exchange & Mart*, so I boxed it up and sent it to Scotland for repair. When I got it back, it was refitted, but it only lasted a few months before it gave trouble again. By this time a new local garage repair business had opened, so I took the car to them.

They contacted Jowett Engineering Ltd in Birstall, Batley, who rebuilt it for me. At the same time I had the brakes relined and new piston rings fitted. Soon after this the car failed its MOT due to a track rod end. This entailed another letter to Jowetts for a spare one. Whilst I was 'awaiting spares' an enthusiast asked me where the car was. He came round and adjusted the ball joint and the car then passed the MOT, so the track rod end was never used!

I was back on the road again, but after a short time the fan came off its shaft and hit the radiator. I must have driven about twenty miles with quite a bad water leak. Father's engineering firm came to my aid again, brazed-up and balanced-up the fan as well as possible. I was also learning how to take things apart and put them together again. We had a few more happy months together until one day when the Javelin's suspension seemed very stiff on one front side. The chassis had broken and according to my garage repairman, it was where the suspension strut was fitted. As he was at an MOT garage, he said he was not prepared to weld in this area as it might prove to be unsafe.

This was about the end of 1963 and I had now got engaged to be married and had taken out a mortgage on a house, so money was now tight. I advertised the Javelin for sale in *Exchange & Mart* for £50. I was inundated with offers, one man came from London on the back of a scooter, then drove my Jowett away!

I don't know why it is, but my wife and I both still have fond memories of our Jowett Javelin, even though it was nothing but trouble. I am sorry there is not much technical detail in this letter, but at that age it was just a car and I am sorry to say I don't even remember its registration number.

B. Bassett, Calne, Wilts

ALL STEEL
and new right through

. The new 1½ litre Javelin has the distinction
of being the first 1947 British car of *wholly new design*
fully tooled for all-steel quantity production.
It will be ready shortly for world-wide distribution.
The British car for which people here
and overseas have been waiting. Price and full
specification will be announced in May.

You're going to like the

Jowett JAVELIN

JOWETT CARS LIMITED, BRADFORD AND LONDON

NHU 971

I owned a Javelin for about three years between 1961 and 1964; it was a black de luxe model with beige leather trim and was registered NHU 971. It was a later model with the two-piece aluminium grille and the 7in headlights. I bought it second-hand from North Taunton in Devon. I parted with it as it started using an alarming amount of oil. I in fact traded it in against a new Mini.

Alfred Trimby, Taunton, Devon

PKM 263

I purchased my Javelin, registered PKM 263, from the Jowett agents Cooter & Green in Beckhenham, Kent, in 1960. I had told them that I was looking for a Javelin and was happy to wait until the right car came in. She was a 1953 de luxe model in black with a dark tan interior. I was the second owner of this well-cared-for example of the marque with some 40,000 miles on the clock.

My Javelin was always a 'working car', and used for daily commuting and leisure trips, and yes, club level competitions. I took part in rallies, driving tests (round a marked-

The Javelin of Alfred Trimby, registered NHU 971, owned by him between 1961 and 1964. These pictures were taken on the day he sold the car in 1964. He traded it in for a Mini.

out course, not the DoT sort), also as a course marshal. PKM 263 had the odd 'after-meeting thrash' around Oulton Park and Thruxton Circuits (the only perk of marshalling in those days). I was competing against Sunbeam Rapiers, MGs, Healy Spridgets, TRs and other typical motor club fare. Despite itsadvancing years, my Javelin generally acquitted itself well.

The car was a late Series 3 model; I had done my homework prior to buying it, as I wanted a car with the oval web crank, but yes, I still managed to break it! Ironically not in competitions, but at about 40mph during moderate road use. I was forced to drive about five miles after the initial 'bang', and even started it again the following morning (which speaks volumes for the compact flat-four layout). When I stripped the engine down, the fracture was the web between No.1 and 2 cylinders. And you have guessed it; the engine had a flat web crank! *Caveat Emptor*, the only sure way to get an oval web engine was if it bore the suffix RO (reconditioned oval).

Cooter & Green were, by this time, Peugeot dealers, but managed to find an oval web at the corner of their workshop. It had been reground three times, but a light skim and new bearings got me out of trouble.

Towards the end of my ownership, in the late 1960s, the engine was suffering from severe erosion of the alloy block water jackets and the top of the alloy block face. I had always used 'Bluecol' antifreeze, so whether this was due to contaminants in the alloy castings, I do not know. It made the measurement of cylinder liner 'nip-up' almost impossible. Water leaks developed, and a crack appeared on the underside of the LH block. By this time I thought I knew Javelin engines inside out, but it was becoming a liability, and the car had to go.

When I bought the Javelin, much had been spoken of the crankshaft problems. I was, however, completely unaware of the gearbox difficulties, but I was about to find out! I broke a tooth off the 1st/reverse layshaft pinion during a driving test. I managed to get a correct ratio (there had been a change in the first gear ratio) cluster, and rebuilt the box with new bearings and bushes. The same problem occurred under far more benign circumstances some two years later. In hindsight I believe that there was a production with the root hardening of some layshaft gear clusters.

I lost count of how many times I had to detach the propshaft, to enable [me] to tow the car when the gearbox 'locked up'. A fellow Javelin owner and I used to take turns to call one another out and assist stripping and juggling the selectors to get the box working again, but we never fully resolved the problem.

The exhaust was not a particular weakness, but they eventually go on any car! My problem was finding a replacement that fitted. Even in the 1960s pattern parts were rife, and in my experience poorly made. I ended up cutting the flanges off an old exhaust and assembling a homemade system using large bore copper pipe and Jubilee clips. It worked well and sounded marvellous, but some of my friends jokingly said that there was more copper pipe in PKM 263 than in a public convenience!

As regards the bodywork, I am sure I have nothing new to report here, as mine was like most people's cars. The trailing edge of the front wings, leading edge of the rear's, and concealed running boards (sills) was were mine went. I did not get rust round the headlamps, where I have seen other Javelins go.

I did get some other miscellaneous troubles, which included brake fade under 'hard use' and experimented with different 'Ferodo' lining compounds. Sorry, I cannot remember now which grade I found was the best. I never had any problems with the notorious internal induction balance pipe. New 'O' rings with a good smear of Hermetite served me well.

There was a design fault on the Javelin heater; the water return bypassed the thermostat. This was a fairly simple modification for warmer feet: Drill one of the external cylinder block/cylinder head and water transfer ports, a suitable size, and braze or weld a stub pipe on. Connect the heater return to this, and blank or seal the original return stub. If there is anyone out there who does not know this mod, I can assure you it transforms things in winter.

I was a member of The Southern Jowett Car Club, and still have the light and dark blue badge in my garage. The honorary president at the time was Marcel Bequart of Le Mans Jupiter fame. I hope that I give no offence to anyone who might have been a member in the early 1960s, but I was a little disappointed with the club then. Most of the meetings were in Buckinghamshire, the few I made the long journey to attend were populated (then less than ten years after production) by what I term Sunday afternoon posing vehicles and owners. Mine was the only day-to-day working car, which was slightly frowned upon. There was little or no technical exchange (with all of the above-mentioned problems, this would have been most helpful for everyone) nor was there the camaraderie I look for in a club.

From the little I have gleaned to date, your club seems to be in a far healthier state now than it was forty years ago! Congratulations. Despite all of my problems, I still think that the Javelin was a wonderful car!

Rex Squires, Orpington, Kent

[*Prior to the war there had been several Jowett Clubs including Northern, Southern and Midlands. After the war however, only The Southern Jowett Car Club remained, which had a strong bias to the South.*

This was the view of many club members in the early 1960s, and so at the club's AGM in 1964 it was agreed that the word 'Southern' should be dropped, so since that time the club has been known as The Jowett Car Club. The club has now grown to a membership of 600 and caters for all Jowett owners in this country and overseas. NS]

Aden

I was serving with the RAF, and was posted to Aden in November 1955. In about February 1956 a colleague and I bought a second-hand Javelin from a local Arab, paying £50 for it. We would have sold it about eighteen months later for £40.

Driving in Aden in the late 1950s was very pleasurable due mainly to the roads having light traffic most of the time, especially the road from RAF Khormaksar to the main town of Steamer Point. At night the road between the town and the camp was virtually devoid of traffic, apart from the odd camel carts carrying their loads. These were driven by owners fast asleep on top of their carts, obviously knowing their camels knew where to go. Because there was so little traffic about at night, many of us young airmen, after having a few drinks in the local bars, would on occasions organise time-spaced races back to camp. (On reflection a very silly thing to do, but at the time great fun.)

My Jowett Javelin won its first race and came second to a Humber Super Snipe in another. I only raced on these two occasions. Another first-time driving experience in Aden was being introduced to giving way to traffic on the right at roundabouts. There were not many roundabouts in Aden, but I believe it was where the British Government first tested the idea – but I could be wrong!

My Javelin became quite well known after I became the Chief Controller of AFBA – the local Forces Broadcasting Service. When

Roy Williams with his Javelin in Aden in 1955. This picture was taken in the compound at RAF Khormaksar.

Another picture of Roy Williams' Javelin in Aden. This picture was taken outside the NAFFI with a Standard Vanguard.

on evening duty it meant I had to travel in and out of the Camp Security Compound where the radio station was situated. The Compound guards got so used to seeing me coming and going in my Javelin they used to wave me straight through. On occasions, although not an officer, I got the odd salute! (Or were they really saluting my Jowett Javelin?!)

My Jowett certainly gave me much driving pleasure, especially when going to the beach at Elephant Bay to swim, and where the WRAF girls would always like to talk to the lads who had nice cars – happy days!

Roy C. Williams, Stretford, Manchester

[*This was a particularly interesting letter from Roy as very few Javelins were sold new to Aden. I have checked the Jowett factory records, which confirm only seven were exported there, so even when Roy had it in 1957 it will have been a rare beast! NS*]

To the bitter end

My father, George Green, joined Jowett Cars Ltd from the Army in November 1945, and was with them until the bitter end at Howden Clough, Birstall, in 1964. He was the service manager for Jowett, and of course we had a Javelin for many years. The one we had was a maroon de luxe model. I have to say, I hated driving it, as I could never start it! Father died in 1990 aged ninety.

Audery Kilburn (née Green), Bradford

George Green and Charles Callcott-Reilly (the chairman of Jowetts) with an early Javelin, registered FKU 372, on a sales trip to Geneva. The picture was sent to me by Mr Green's daughter, Audrey, who said her father ran a Javelin for many years, right into the 1960s.

The Javelin of Mrs Moss, registered OPP 771, being raced by her. This picture was originally published in Motor Sport *in 1954. The caption reads: 'Moss Trophy Trial, the competitor is Mrs N.H. Moss in her Javelin.' This was one of five driving tests during the trial, organised by the Harrow CC. Her son, Sir Stirling Moss, told me in his letter that they had published her initials wrongly, they should have been N.A. Moss. (I am most grateful to* Motor Sport *for giving me permission to use this picture.)*

Favourite car

I learnt to drive in my father's Jowett Javelin in York, prior to moving to Scarborough; I would have been about seventeen at the time. He had several cars, including a Lanchester and a Jaguar. Of all the cars I drove of his, plus the cars I have owned since, the Javelin has to be my favourite.

It was a dark green de luxe example with beige leather trim and a wooden dashboard. I remember the engine was very flat, my father said that was because the pistons went from side to side, rather than the usual up-and-down-type engine! [*Yes – the Javelin had a flat-four horizontally-opposed engine. NS*]

I have now been driving for fifty-four years and have owned eleven VWs, my latest one being a Passat Estate.

Mrs Judy Bradley, Scarborough

[*Judy has been in correspondence with me for several years now, and regularly sends me items of Jowett interest – thank you Judy. NS*]

Stirling Moss

My mother had a Jowett Javelin and I remember that we all thought it was a good alternative to the Lancia Aprilla, which also was a nice machine. I think I probably drove the car but not in any sort of competition.

Very regrettably, I haven't got the time, memory, or talent to write a piece on the car – I'm not a journalist! However, if you want to mention that the family did have one and liked it very much, this would certainly not be out of order.

Sir Stirling Moss

another success for Jowett's!

—this time at Le Mans with the new

JAVELIN *JUPITER*

In the Le Mans International 24-hour Sports Car Race the only Javelin Jupiter entered gained 1st place in the 1½-litre class breaking the class record at an average speed for the whole 24-hour Race of 77·1 m.p.h. This is the first time the Jupiter has entered a race. The car was driven by Mr. T. H. Wisdom and Mr. T. C. Wise.

Subject to official confirmation

JOWETT CARS LIMITED · BRADFORD AND LONDON

4 The Jupiter
The car that won at Le Mans three times!

NYW 715

In August 1956 I was transferred, on loan, from my parent establishment in Lancashire to a sister establishment in Berkshire. I was to marry in the October and had sold my two-litre SA model MG and had a 250cc Panther motorcycle as my means of transport.

Motorcycling was not my favourite way of getting about and I had a desire for an MG TC but my purse would not stretch that far. I could, however, afford a Jupiter and, as one was available privately in Reading for £350 cash, I became the proud owner of a black with red leather interior Jowett Jupiter, a 1951 SA model, registration number NYW 715. Unfortunately, after a very promising start, the car suffered a cracked crankshaft. Welding by Bucklers of Reading did not prove entirely satisfactory (days before Argon Arc, etc. was in common use). About this time my wife and I moved back to Lancashire and, in the summer of 1957, a new crankcase was purchased and fitted.

The car performed well for the remainder of 1957 and the first six months of 1958. We had decided that we would have a continental touring holiday in the August of that year and planned to visit Rome, seeing as much as we could on the way there and back. Those were the days when you could only take £50 out of the country, so we planned to camp for the majority of the nights and only use hotels in the cities.

We left Leyland in Lancashire and drove to Newhaven for the overnight crossing to Dieppe, no 'roll-on roll-off' ferries then from this port. The car was hoisted up by crane and deposited in the bowels of the boat. Our route through France was: Paris, Lyon, Avignon, Cannes and Monte Carlo. We crossed into Italy on the coast road and continued on through Genoa, La Spezia and Pisa to Rome. So far the car had performed perfectly, not missing a beat.

For our return journey we drove north from Rome through Florence, Bologna, Venice, into the Dolomites to Cortina then back down to Milan and into Switzerland via Como. Some fifty miles into Switzerland, in the centre of a small town called Chur, we broke down, no gears at all. A traffic police-man enquired of our inability to move and sent for a garage recovery vehicle. The column gear change shaft had partially sheared. The garage allowed me to effect a repair using their workshop facilities, and were keen for their apprentices to look the Jupiter over since it was an unfamiliar model to them.

Back on the road after two or three hours, our route took us through Lucerne, Interlaken and Bern. Once again the gear change gave up the ghost and roadside repairs were necessary. Eventually I could engage all forward gears but not reverse, so we continued on our way with no reverse, and it is surprising how often one needs to reverse.

We pressed on into France, through Besançon, Reims and St Quentin to Arras. By the time we had reached Arras, French

Mr Hardisty's Juptiter, NYM 715, at Preston railway station, ready for towing home after breaking a crank on holiday in Switzerland, which required recovery back to England by the RAC. The car was black with a red leather trim and was bought in 1956 for £350.

roads had taken their toll on the centre prop-shaft bearing/coupling; severe vibration came in at about 35mph. We stayed the night in Arras and the local garage did what was necessary to enable us to reach Calais and a boat back to the UK. The journey from Dover was uneventful and we felt that we had had a holiday to remember.

The winter of 1958/59 was spent putting NYW 718 to rights including a crankshaft re-grind and fitting new bearings, etc. When I bought the car my boss warned me that in his opinion if I had the crankshaft re-ground it would break. I was going to remember that comment sometime in the future.

For our 1959 holiday we felt confident in our ability to tour the Continent again and our destination this year was going to be Vienna. We would travel to Dover and use the new-fangled 'roll-on roll-off' ferry to Ostend. Our route to Austria would be through Belgium, Luxembourg, Germany and Switzerland. We entered Germany at Saarbrucken and, by the time we reached Karlsruhe, had suffered a broken steering gear member. This happened as we were passing a large heavy-goods vehicle garage. They undertook to do a welding job immediately for us and within a couple of hours we were on our way as good as new.

In Switzerland we drove through Zurich, Lucerne, Interlaken and then Chur. Were we tempting fate visiting the same place where we had had problems last year? After Chur we bypassed a small village called Lanquart. As we passed the village it happened! I heard a sharp crack followed by a loud bang and I knew immediately that the crankshaft had broken. I remembered my boss's warning. We left the car by the roadside and walked down an embankment into the village where we found a VW garage. It was Saturday afternoon but the owner was there so we explained our problem to him; he could not have been more helpful. He arranged to tow the Jupiter to his garage and to take us and our camping equipment to a nearby camp-site. On the Monday I returned to the garage to examine the engine and decide what to do next. Fortunately we had RAC 5 Star Recovery and they, with the garage, arranged recovery to the UK. We stayed a couple more days in Lanquart then returned to Leyland by train and ferry.

Some three or four weeks later the Jupiter was delivered to Preston Station rather the worse for wear. The hood was torn and various pieces of equipment that we had been forced to leave with the car were either vandalised or missing – fortunately we were able to prove that the damage had been done on British Rail and eventually received adequate compensation. My wife and a colleague collected the car and towed it to our home near Leyland. Within a few weeks I had located a crankshaft in Leeds, collected it complete with bearings and re-assembled the engine; the car was once again road-worthy.

We had been proud owners of a Jupiter for almost three years but we needed some-thing more reliable as we two were about to become three, so we traded it in for our first new car, either a Ford Anglia or Austin A40, whichever came first, and by Easter 1960 we had a new green Austin A40

A.A. Hardisty, Salisbury

GPY 859

I owned a very pretty special-bodied Jupiter, registration GPY 859, from 1953 to 1955. It was second-hand when I bought it and I sold it to another enthusiast in the Jowett Car Club. His name was Mr Hocker and I recall a year later receiving a postcard from him, out of the blue, from Italy, telling me that he and his wife were touring Europe on holi-day and the Jupiter was performing perfectly

and how pleased they were with it. It looked rather like a smaller XK120 Jag and had a large (for those days) flat-raked windscreen, not the split-V windscreen of the standard Jupiter. It had a bench seat and I seem to remember a steering column gear change. It was black with green upholstery. I have very happy memories of that car and often won-der what happened to it. I recall vague rumours at the time that they were prone to crankshaft failures but I never had any trou-ble with the car of any sort.

I do vaguely recall that the previous owner to me was a titled gentleman and the name of Sir Hugh Bell does – if you'll pardon the pun – ring a bell! I guess he would have been the first owner because I don't think it had many miles on the clock when I bought it in 1953. I was a member of the Jowett Car Club then (and a local car club) and entered my Jupiter in several driving tests and minor rallies.

This pretty special-bodied Jupiter was built by Lionel Rawson for its first owner, Sir Hugh Bell, and regis-tered GPY 859. It was bought by Michael Smyth in 1953, and is seen here at a Jowett Car Club event at Chessington Zoo in the mid-1950s.

Two views of the Jupiter, registered BDJ 905, owned by Frank Lennon. These pictures were taken on his honeymoon trip, which took him and his new bride as far as San Remo in Italy.

The car was built by Lionel Rawson, a firm of coachbuilders, [and] I was intrigued to learn that the car is still in existence – and in Surrey. If and when it is restored and road-worthy, I'd love to see it sometime. Happy memories!

I now drive a sedate Citroen Xantia 2.0i.
Michael Smyth, Godstone, Surrey

BDJ 905

I owned a Jowett Jupiter, registered BDJ 905, between 1953 and 1954. I went on my honeymoon in the car and got as far as San Remo in Italy. I passed it on to a local garage, Maclean & Appleton, who are not now in existence. It was bought by a young man who was in the RAF in the south of England, who wrote to me after buying it. I thought it was a really nice car but had one or two problems with it, such as the petrol pump freezing-up in the winter as it was under the chassis and exposed to the elements.

It had those awful steering column gear levers, which caused it to get stuck in second gear at times. I have to say, however, performance-wise and road holding-wise I was very keen on it.

I saw Jupiters race in the Isle of Man in the TT about that time. We went to see Geoff Duke, who was from down the road here; he was driving an Aston Martin.

Frank Lennon, St Helens, Merseyside

980 AMC

From approximately 1962 to 1965 I owned a Jowett Jupiter with the registration number 980 AMC. It was one of the last without a separate boot lid and had some of the modifications already which would be officially introduced with the revised model with boot lid.

The car had been fitted, before I bought it, with an oval web crank engine and had a history of breaking gearboxes. I eventually used Javelin boxes and rebuilt from a pile of spares as they broke. An engine oil cooler had been fitted by the previous owner and I fitted an ex-aircraft engine oil temperature gauge. The car had been fitted by a previous owner with a back axle crown-wheel-and-pinion from one of the Le Mans cars, this gave it a much lighter gearing than standard, but the speedo had not been modified to suit. [*I wish I could confirm this! NS*]

During my ownership, I had a minor accident to the offside front, which was enough to break the nearside front chassis tube, which extended forwards from the main frame to support the engine. I had a new tube section rolled to fit inside the tube and had this welded in with no adverse effects. I had the occasional problem with oil in the cooling water due to my incorrectly fitting the head gasket water seals, but again this was

This special-bodied Jupiter, chassis number 46, was built in Sri Lanka and was a four-seater with running boards. The picture was taken in Sri Lanka in 1955 and was sent to me by the owner of the MG, the Jupiter happened to be next to his car when this picture was taken. I am glad it was, as this is the only pictorial evidence we have of this car, which was scrapped in Sri Lanka many years ago.

This pretty little Jupiter coupé was owned by Margaret Jenkins and her late husband in the late 1950s. The car was chassis number EO/SA/35 and was the sole fixed-head coupé built by Lionel Rawson. It was delivered to the Jowett agents J. Gilder & Co., Sheffield, on 17 November 1950. Sadly the car seems to have been lost after an accident in 1966; this is the only known picture of this unique car.

easily overcome. I once lost the passenger door in a very high wind; it was blown open and the hinges (cast aluminium) broke off. I had them re-welded in the aircraft engine factory where I worked. The handbrake lever was very weak and made from 'bent tin' – it broke across the cable nipple hole. I believe I managed to get a new replacement for it, as Barnett & Small's Garage in Farnham, Surrey, still maintained a stock of spares in those days. One breakdown was caused by a piston top detaching itself from the piston skirt – no real damage was done and I fitted a new set of pistons without re-boring the cylinders.

Carburettor icing was always a problem, as was water getting onto the spark plugs despite rubber shields. Various people fitted spark plugs and leads from military vehicles, which were fully shielded and waterproofed, but despite working by then at a tank research establishment, I never carried out this modification. When I owned it, the car was painted British Racing Green and had tan leather seating. I fitted a black leather-padded dashboard cover over the original, rather tatty, wood finish. The car had as an accessory a home-made fibreglass hardtop for winter use; this had minimal headroom, even for someone only 5ft 5in tall, but gave a very low and streamlined look.

As a youngster with a sports car, I did not look after it as well as perhaps I should have and eventually part-exchanged it for an Armstrong Siddeley Sapphire 234, which was much more powerful and even rarer than the Jowett.

In all, I thoroughly enjoyed my experiences with the Jupiter and regretted selling it. Where is it now? Is it still existing? Can you tell me?

Roger Speak, Aldershot, Hants

[*Sorry Roger, I have no record of 980 AMC, the closest I can get is 977 AMC – this is on a car that is still alive and well! NS*]

LWT 478 and NXH 439

My involvement with Jowett started in May 1952, when I bought a new Javelin, registered LWT 478, from the Jowett agents Glovers of Ripon. This was a very nice car.

The only problem I had was with the carburettors; they would ice up in freezing fog, as they were stuck out on a limb. I had a serious crash in this car which bent the entire bodywork, so I eventually part-exchanged it for a second-hand Jupiter, registered NXH 439.

The Jupiter was great fun to drive, but after some considerable use the crankshaft broke in two, but the engine would still tick over. I went on my honeymoon in the car to France and Switzerland, and it proved to be most reliable.

Having bought a farm, I reluctantly had to sell the Jupiter, trading it in for an Austin A40 Countryman, which was a bit of a change! I now run a Mitsubishi Space Star, which I really like; plenty of room and all mod cons!

Peter Godlee, Bedale, North Yorkshire

HKW 610

My Jowett Jupiter was registered HKW 610. I bought it from Performance Cars, on the Great West Road in west London, in the late spring of 1955 and I think I paid £425 for it. I was an undergraduate at Cambridge at the time, so made full use of it there. I hill-climbed it once at Craigantlet in the summer of 1955 or 1956, but found the new MGAs too fast and I was not prepared to bend my car.

During my national service I took it to Aldershot when I was at Mons Officer Cadet School and it proved very useful in getting up to London and back late at night, even with black-market petrol because the Suez Crisis was on.

When I was posted to Sennelager in Germany I took it with me, and I had no trouble with it in getting around until I lent it to a brother officer who wrapped it round a concrete kilometre post on ice. It took some time to mend and from that moment I was never quite so sure of it. I was demobbed after one year in Germany and

This lovely picture of a Jupiter, registered NLX 901, was sent to me by S. Stonard. It was a picture he took of his old friend in his new Jupiter, sadly his friend died some years ago. The car still exists and is owned by club members Keith and Pauline Winteringham.

Betty and Stanley Boyd bought this Jupiter, registered LTM 445, in September 1952. It was coloured ivory with red leather trim.

drove it home over snow-bound autobahns with no problem. Being short of cash and not sure of the car, I sold it for cash to a street trader off the Tottenham Court Road. I bought a Minor 1000.

I loved the car, I would love to know more about it. I knew that the Le Mans team cars were HKW registration, [but] I never knew if mine had any association with the team. It had the lovely gurgle of a flat-four and, while I did not get the resonance of a TR-two in acceleration, I knew it had roadholding second to none.

Patrick D. Montgomery, Holywood, Co. Down

[*Sorry Patrick, HKW was a Bradford registration, and yes HKWs were on some of the Le Mans cars, but yours was not one of them. NS*]

Another view of LTM 445, parked next to another Jupiter, registered LMJ 517, plus a view of LMJ 517 on its own.

LTM 445

My husband Stanley and I bought a Jowett Jupiter in August/September 1952 and it was the pride and joy of our life. After so many bleak years of war and its aftermath, it was wonderful to own a sports car again.

Our model was registered LTM 445 and was white with scarlet upholstery and hood and radio and cigar lighter! We later had a red tonneau cover specially made at a mews workshop near Marble Arch and an Esso

Tiger's head was painted on the driver's door. I believe it was 1954 when the crankshaft broke (on the A1) and we had extensive repairs. My husband died over twenty years ago, but he would have been able to give you all the mechanical details of the car.

Our beloved 'Jupy' was the car of our dreams – there has never been another car so elegant and stylish.

Betty Boyd, Bournemouth

Army trips

On my brother John's advice, I bought my Jowett Jupiter in late 1956 or early 1957 on my return from Army service in Korea, Japan and Cyprus. I was then stationed in Chatham and must have bought the car in London, but I cannot remember from whom or where, but I know it cost me £600, which was a lot of money in those days. I must have saved the money whilst on my three years' overseas service! This was not my first car because I bought a 1925/26 Austin Chummy in 1947 for £50, and gave it away in 1951 – a pity I did not hang onto it!

The Jupiter was in British Racing Green and was a super car. As a mountaineer I used it a lot with Army friends in North Wales, and on Sunday trips from Chatham to the rock outcrops near Tunbridge Wells. I sometimes took it up to town and could put on quite a speed along the old A2 from Rochester to Blackheath. I do not remember ever doing 100mph, but must have got very close to it on a number of times. I believe that John Blashford-Snell, in one of his books where he mentions the Jupiter, boasts about doing the ton!

John was at Chatham with me as a young officer (2nd Lt) and I was Adjutant; I think he lived in the other Mess at Chatham as his Y.O. course was split between our two units for living accommodation. I cannot say that I remember him or his Jupiter at Chatham, being administered by the other regiment with whom he lived.

I only used the Jupiter for about eighteen months before I was sent to Kenya for two years; I stored the car at a garage in Weymouth. In 1960 I was posted to Germany and found I was not able to insure the Jupiter there, so I had to sell it for £200 – what a loss!

Major E.M. Warrick FRGS RE (retd),
Montacute, Somerset

PWB 208

Some time ago I met Noel Stokoe at Pickering with a Jowett Jupiter, and as I had one in 1955 to 1961, registered PWB 208, we got talking and he asked me to write about my experience of breaking a crankshaft in France in 1957.

Well, I bought my Jupiter in 1955 for £645 (instead of a house) against my wife's wishes; I really fell in love with this car in the showroom.

When I bought the car I always dried it off after the rain before I went to bed. I don't really know why I sold it but I did, in 1961, for £315 with 34,000 miles on the clock and in perfect condition. I decided to go to France in 1957 with my wife and a friend of mine just out of the army. I fitted a special chrome luggage rack to the car as luggage space was limited and we went camping to France. Fifteen miles south of Lyon, on the old RN7, a loud rattle came from the engine. After checking the engine I found the front pulley on the crankshaft moved backwards and forwards; I realised the crankshaft was broken. I knew the Jupiter had a reputation for a weak crankshaft. To say we were sick was an understatement.

While we were thinking what to do a Mercedes suddenly pulled up, driven by a British Army officer. He had seen my friend's blazer badge (Royal Engineers) and, as he was a major in the Engineers, offered to tow us to the nearest garage, which turned out to be a very small village (sixty inhabitants) – there he left us. The garage owner – typical Frenchman in denims and beret – had a look at the car and said he had never seen or heard of a Jowett and would not be able to get parts, so that was that. That night we stayed in a small hotel in the village, £4 for dinner, bed and breakfast each, quite expensive as wages in England were around £9 to £10 per week.

This page and overleaf:
*Four pictures of the Jupiter,
registered PWB 208,
owned by Ron Whitfield.
These pictures were taken
in 1957 on a trip to the
South of France. Sadly he
broke a crank on the way
down, but as he was in the
RAC they flew one out for
him. He fitted it and continued on his holiday!*

Going to the garage next morning, a small circus was filling up with petrol and I had a conversation with a lady who spoke very good English. She said she would have a word with the garage owner after I told her I was a mechanic and would try to get a crank from England. As she was French and my French was limited, she persuaded him to let me try to sort the car out myself, but I had to be out of the garage by Monday. It was now Wednesday. I was a member of the RAC so the next thing was to get in touch with them. They were affiliated to Automobile Club de France but the ACF was in Lyon and I had to get there.

After trying unsuccessfully to thumb a lift I tried the old trick of letting my wife stand in shorts and thumb one. It worked, and I suddenly turned up – the French driver took it in good part and not only took us to the ACF in Lyon but waited to see if we had any success. The ACF rang Paris and Nice to see if anyone had a crankshaft, for there were a few agencies in France for Jowetts as Javelins had done well in the Monte Carlo Rally. Jupiters had done well at Le Mans in recent years, but we had no luck so they let me ring the RAC in London, who said they would send one on the first available flight.

We returned to the village by bus and with the help of my friend, who really knew little about motor cars, removed the engine and then the broken crankshaft. One of our problems was solved when a farmer's wife opposite the garage said as we had camping gear we could camp on their land free. We are still friends with these people and stay with their daughter when we visit France. If your French is limited it is very difficult to use the phone, so I had two trips to Lyon airport to see if the crank had arrived. This was quite an experience on the local bus, calling at all the small villages, picking up people with piglets, bicycles, pushchairs, boxes of fruit, all put on the roof. It took one hour fifteen minutes to do around eighteen miles. The crank arrived on Saturday, three days after ringing the RAC. When I examined the crankshaft it was different to the old one, but I remembered reading about a new balanced laystall shaft being made (oval webs) and this was one. Anyway back to the village; everything was ready to put in the crank. By Sunday lunchtime the engine was running; the only mistake I made was fitting the oil pump which put the ignition timing out, this was rectified by changing the HT leads and moving the body of the distributor. The crankshaft was £32, freight £1 17s 6d (£1.87 ½p) to be paid on return to England. So off we went to the south of France, only losing five days out of twenty-one days' holiday and paying the garage £5 for oil, paraffin, gasket, cement, etc. As the crankshaft was imported free of duty, we were supposed to bring the old one in two pieces back to customs: we had the two pieces stuck in the ground when we were camping with the notice on – *souvenir de vacances*.

I hope this has been interesting and wish I still had the Jupiter. Luckily I kept the other car I had at the same time, a rare Vauxhall Limousine BXL Conaught 27hp (1936), which I hope to have on the road again this year after standing in my workshop since 1962.

Ron Whitfield, Doncaster

I owned a Jupiter in 1964, it was registered PWB 208. [*This car was owned by Ron Whitfield a little earlier – see his letter, above. What a coincidence! NS*] It was the most beautiful car ever to come into my possession. At the time I was living in Doncaster, and my father contacted me as it had failed to reach its reserve price at a car auction in Bawtry. We rushed back to the auction in my Vauxhall Velox to successfully negotiate a straight swap, my old Velox for his Jupiter!

Gordon Pott owned this Jupiter, registered HKW 918, from September 1958 to June 1959. He had no mechanical problems with the car, but sold it as he needed a larger boot space.

I was eighteen at the time and had picked up the Velox on my round, working as a coalman. I had fitted small ends and done a lot of work to the bodywork of the Velox, but it was with some trepidation when I made the swap, as the purchaser was a foreman at the local Vauxhall agency!

He told me it had been fitted with the latest Laystall crank, after the original broke on the Monte Carlo Rally. I have no idea as to whether this was correct or not, but the car had been abroad and had a lot of extra lights fitted. [*No, it was fitted by Ron Whitfield, see his letter above. NS*]

An insurance agent, on seeing the Jupiter told me that this was the model that broke the Jowett Co. with its development costs. He also said one turned over, killing the driver whilst on high-speed trials at the MIRA track.

In my opinion the Javelin and Jupiter were both years ahead of their time and it was a great shame when production ceased.

Robin James Concah, Torquay, Devon

[*Robin did not send me any photos of the car, as I don't think he had any. However I am sure he will like the ones that Ron sent in, which are featured in the book. Sadly I do not know the fate of this car, but I do not think that it has survived. NS*]

HKW 918

I once owned a Jowett Jupiter, which was registered HKW 918. I only owned it for a short time between 22 September 1958 and 9 June 1959, when I was living at Mellor in Cheshire.

Another Jupiter that was in the area at the time was owned by Roy Braddock of H. Braddock & Son Ltd, engineers of Oldknow Road Garage, Marple, Cheshire.

This Jupiter, registered JVJ 148, was owned by the explorer Colonel John Blashford-Snell; he called the car 'The Green Dragon'. The girl in the car later became his wife, Judith.

This firm was originally based in Stockport Road, Marple, and must have been one of the very earliest Jowett agents in the country, dating from the early 1920s, and were experts in the marque and carried spares for all models of car and van.

Having purchased it second-hand, I took it to Roy Braddock to check it over for me and it gave me good service all the time that I had it. I think I probably changed it due to the small luggage capacity of the boot. I cannot think of any other reason, as I had no problems with the car.

I was very angry at how Jowetts were pushed out of production by the machinations of 'the big boys'. In my opinion the car embodied many features of efficient design, which would still be advanced today. It was a much better car than, say, the Morgan, and look how they are in demand today!

E.G. Pott, Arnside, via Carnforth

JVJ 148

I had a number of unusual cars (including a BSA Scout, an AC Greyhound and a Bristol 406) but the Jupiter was certainly a favourite.

The registration of the car was JVJ 148, I cannot remember if I ever reached 100mph in the car, but it could certainly motor! I wonder if she is still around?

I have just been in Ethiopia, preparing for an expedition with older people who still feel young at heart. My old pal Tim Nicholson got me to lead the crossing of the infamous Darien Gap in Range Rovers in 1972. I've written up a number of my motoring experiences in *Something Lost Behind the Ranges* (Harper Collins) which most libraries have, or it is available in paperback.

Colonel John Blashford-Snell OBE

The incredible styling on this Jupiter was done by Jack Smith in Tasmania. I love things that are one-offs or unusual, and find that this car fits the bill on both counts!

The Black Concertina – A Tune with a Jupiter

Seated in a four-gallon drum in his extensive corrugated iron workshop, Jack Smith was totally absorbed in playing a small black concertina. He appeared not to notice me as I poked about amongst partly dismantled farm machinery, trucks, cars, motorcycles, water pumps and engines. Even a dolly's pram, missing one wheel, was propped against a holed Furphy water cart.

The 1950s concertina tunes had a strangely soothing effect and time seemed of no consequence. Opened packing cases marked 'Jack Smith, Mechanic, Copping,

Tasmania' were stacked along the far wall and here and there on the shelves above were wine glasses, contents unfinished. Finally, I approached close enough for Jack to cease playing, but he remained seated. 'Have a drop of wine,' he said.

With some diffidence I made my pitch. 'John Locke said you were thinking of selling the Jupiter?' In silence he led me to a dark corner and carefully removed the tarpaulin. Words seemed superfluous ... 'I styled it,' he offered, as if sacrilege was a virtue. Perhaps a transformation rather than restoration describes the months of work that followed. Although I was familiar with

Two more views of the same car, after hundreds of hours of work by Jim Pointer, putting the car back into original trim.

Jowett Javelins, it soon became clear that the Jupiter demanded special care and attention.

The tubular steel chassis designed by Johnson & Eberhorst, a marvel of strength and lightness, was meticulously cleaned, checked for rust, cracks and dimensional accuracy, and then coated with a hard finish. Removal of Jack's 'styling' fins and spats left hundreds of holes in the aluminium body panels. That and the fabrication of a new hardtop would require rare skills. Then to the rescue came Tom Roper, ex-RAAF Spitfire-fitter and instructor at the Hobart Technical College. Tediously all the holes and cracks were welded and panels reshaped where necessary. Tom's stories about Spitfires and the Japanese bombing attacks on Darwin and Western Australia during WW2 were a fascinating bonus.

A virgin sheet of panel steel fashioned into the shapely, curved hard top was an artistic miracle. No dies or jigs, just eyes, and hands rolled and drew the complex pieces through a wheel he had made from a steel locomotive tyre. With a rear window from a Humber Hawk, an admirer said it looked like 'a baby Jag'. Although standard suspension with front longitudinal torsion bars and transverse rear was generally satisfactory, the local Javelin club had developed some mod-

Same Stable

JAVELIN

JUPITER

The new Jupiter luggage boot

The Javelin now has the new Series III engine which retains the Javelin's well proved horizontally opposed principle but incorporates the modifications resulting from five years of successful international competition work and from strenuous overseas use. The Jupiter also has the Series III engine tuned for specially high performance — and behind the driver is a roomy tonneau and luggage boot. The Bradford Commercial range— van, utility, and lorry, is known all over the world for its amazing economy and sturdy reliability. These three cars come from the same famous Yorkshire stable of Jowett Cars Limited who have been making cars for nearly half a century.

JOWETT
of BRADFORD

Mrs D. Ingham with the Jupiter she bought new in December 1951. It was bought from the Jowett agents Chester Brothers Ltd, Birmingham. The car was originally coloured copper with red leather trim.

ifications using Australian Holden parts. Front bronze yokes were carefully reamed out, larger bushes fitted and, with other minor changes, handling was distinctly improved and durability extended. After studying William Body's paper on 'Technical development of Javelin and Jupiter flat-four Engines' as published in March 1953's issue of *Motor Sport*, it became clear that an engine rebuild would be desirable. By this time, the immensely strong oval-webbed Laystall crankshaft was available.

We ordered twelve – the other eleven were quickly snapped up locally by knowledgeable Javelin fanciers. With eyes firmly on the main game, namely reliability, very careful attention was given to reassembly. Cleaning of water and oil passages, port polishing and relieving, gasket fit, torsion wrench settings, valve and ignition timing, carburettor tuning and balancing and all electrical wiring and appliances checked. Not least was an accuracy check on the oil temperature gauge, so as not to exceed 75°C (166°F), and replacement of the thermostat. Finally came the difficult decision on body colour. We tried many different shades and combinations, all disappointing. But it was black that looked best. Thank you, Henry Ford.

The first test run was short and sedate. Everything seemed to work and there were no alarming noises or symptoms of malfunction. The second run, with a full load of fuel and a passenger, was over some narrow sealed roads, a stretch of gravel and about 100km of highway. As expected, handling on the country road with tight and often irregular 'radiused' corners was fairly quick and predictable. On gravel the ride was good but, with the short wheelbase, not too many liberties could be taken. Of course, the highway running was the car's natural element and it flew like a little bird. With annual holidays coming up, and two fitted suitcases snugly in the space behind the back seats, the long-wished-for expedition to visit our daughter in Perth was on. But that's another story altogether, 'To the west, by Jupiter!'

N.E. Pointer, Hobart, Tasmania

Footnote: *Hobart (42.53S 147.19E) is about 4,000km from Perth (31.56S 115.50E) by most convenient road route, plus about 400km by ferry across Bass Strait. (Jupiter R1 covered about 3,000km to win 1½ litre class at Le Mans' twenty-four hour race in 1952. NEP.*

My Jupiter, registered JBE 4, taken at an event in Whitby a few years ago. I have owned this car since February 1985.

My car again, this time taken at Goathland (Aidensfield) whilst filming for Heartbeat *in early 1994. Nick Berry was still PC Rowan in those days and is pictured with the car. He was interested in it, as he had not seen a Jowett Jupiter before; he told me he owned an E-type Jag. When the episode was shown, the car was featured for about half a second!*

JBE 4

I was the owner of a Jowett Jupiter JBE 4. It was bought by my father for me, new, in January 1952 from Marshall's Garage Ltd, the Jowett agents in Scunthorpe. Marshall's are still in existence and have been BMW agents for many years. At the time my father bought the car for me, I was doing my national service and was based in Hereford.

I owned the car for about eighteen months, then traded it in at Marshall's for a black Hillman drophead, which was a much more reliable car. During my ownership of JBE 4, I had a lot of trouble with her. The first time I drove the car from Hereford to Scunthorpe, the gear leaver fell off the steering column into my lap!

I was later posted to York, and well remember opening the car up on the York to Tadcaster dual carriageway, travelling at 105mph, when I blew the top off one of the pistons. The garage fitted a new engine, but that had to be removed as there was a major mechanical problem with it. So a third engine was fitted, and ran well for a short time.

I took the car on holiday to Scotland and broke down twenty miles out of Wick and had to be towed back to Inverness for repair. After getting the car back on the road, this was when I thought it was time to switch to a more reliable car. I also had two new hoods fitted whilst the car was in my ownership, as it would rip when I opened it!

I was interested to note the car is now British Racing Green, as it was red with a beige hood and trim when it was new. It is interesting that you can still see the red paint under the green where it has been chipped.

I must say I was amazed that the car was still around, as I have to say it was the most unreliable car I ever owned. I think I must have sorted out all the problems the car had, ready for the second owner!

Richard Jones, Scunthorpe

I do not own a Jupiter, but I believe I can do better than this, as the Jupiter JBE 4 was in my ownership in the early 1960s. At the time I was a youth, strapped for cash, and just wanted some reliable transport. I bought the car from a bombsite dealer for £20.

As I remember, the car was then painted red. It had obviously been stored for some time under cover, as the paintwork was pretty good, except for the back end, which did not fit under the cover. Mechanically the car was not very good; the bearings on the rod that operated the cooling fan were very noisy. The only way I could stop the engine after switching it off was to put it in gear and stall it!

Having the registration JBE 4 was nice as I was always thought to be somebody important. I remember driving into garage forecourts and getting my windscreen cleaned, etc., before I had the chance for a gallon of the cheap! Happy days! – I eventually traded the car in and was allowed £35 for it.

Geoff Foreman, Dhahran, Saudi Arabia

[*These two letters refer to the same car, which is in fact the Jupiter I own – I bought it in 1985. At the time I only knew the car's history from the date in the continuation logbook, which was 1965. I have now been able to fill in most of its history except from late 1953 to 1960. I also found out that it was raced at Goodwood in 1954 by a K.L.W. Cook, but as yet I have not been able to find out who he was. NS*]

BRITISH *JUPITER*
WINS MONTE CARLO RALLY

$1\frac{1}{2}$ *litre class*

the winning Jupiter gets a bouquet.

Sports convertible, gives you highest performance and race-bred handling qualities yet is economical to run.

JOWETT **JUPITER**

Made in Britain by
*JOWETT CARS
LIMITED
Idle, Bradford,
Yorkshire*

Family saloon. Combines luxury with speed and completely manoeuvrable in traffic.

JOWETT **JAVELIN**

In the rough, tough, Monte Carlo Rally last January, Jowett cars, competing against some of the world's finest automobiles, made spectacular wins for Britain:—

- Jupiters were 1st and 2nd in the $1\frac{1}{2}$ litre class.

- The Javelin saloon came 4th in the $1\frac{1}{2}$ litre class.

- Jowett Cars won the coveted Manufacturers Team Prize in the $1\frac{1}{2}$ litre class.

- Jowett Cars shared the Stuart Trophy for the best British performance.

SEE AND BUY THESE CARS AT:

THE HOFFMAN MOTOR CO. INC., 487 PARK AVENUE, NEW YORK 22, U.S.A.
ANGELL MOTORS, 1145 SOUTH FAIR OAKS, PASADENA 2, CALIFORNIA.
SANDERS MOTOR SALES, 3005 WASHINGTON AVENUE, HOUSTON, TEXAS.

These distributors or your dealer can have a Javelin or a Jupiter waiting for you in England for your 1951 vacation.

5 Memories of the CD

Jowett's 'last throw of the dice'

Part One

Following Steve Waldenberg's plea in the *Jowetteer* for CD memories, I fell to thinking about the various phases of the CD development programme. Once I started to recall things and events I began to realise that, since duration testing was one of my functions within the Experimental Department of Jowett Cars, I had handled all variants of the model. The more I thought about it, the more I realised there may be the basis of an article or two, so, in the hope that a few memories are stirred and a few recollections refurbished, here goes.

It must be remembered of course that the passing of fifty years does tend to cloud things and some memories may be a little scanty in recall.

My first association with the CD range was GKY 540, the 'Tram'. This was, by any standards, an over-bodied six-seater. It was the first attempt to put a body onto the completely new chassis, which had been evolved for the CD range. You must bear in mind that the CC Bradford had a ladder-type frame with semi-elliptic springs to both front and rear axles. The front axle was a solid beam, as all its predecessors had been. Under the bonnet was the well-revered side valve flat-twin with the cast aluminium combined water and inlet tract. Upon this was mounted the single downdraught carburettor with extremely basic choke control by means of a flat metal plate which was drawn across the

open inlet orifice. The three-speed floor change gearbox transmitted power to the back axle and was, to be kind, rather slow in operation. In fact, you counted between the gears, otherwise you'd beat the change. The steering was ... well you aimed it, you didn't steer it!

Imagine the total difference, both in technology and handling, with the CD chassis. Here was a real leap forward. A cruciform frame which only has semi-elliptic at the rear, independent front suspension off the Javelin and telescopic shock absorbers all round. What a difference to the ride characteristics. Still a flat-twin, but overhead inlet and side exhaust, and one carb per pot. Roy Lunn, as architect of the project, really did do the very best he possibly could on an extremely limited budget. The power was transmitted through a newly designed four-speed gearbox – how sophisticated. Altogether a totally different base for what was, in many respects, a range of vehicles well ahead of their time. Imagine: one chassis and four different bodies. A motoring Meccano set! But I get ahead of myself.

In order to test the first rolling chassis, the 'Tram' was built. The body was fabricated in Experimental Department by those wizards of the panel hammer, under the direction of Bill Poulter. One of them was Bill Egglestone, I remember. Nicknamed Big Eggo after the cartoon in the *Beano* comic of the day. In order to get something on the road, it was very sensible to keep costs in

Two views of the CD Estate car, registered HKW 272 on test, driven a large proportion of the time by Phill Green.

check by using as many standard components from current production. Therefore, the chassis stood on Javelin wheels and tyres. The front bumper was Javelin; the scuttle and windscreen, front wings and front doors were also Javelin. There were actually four doors but, even though it was an estate car-type body, there was no rear opening into a rear load space. This was not really surprising, since the whole of the interior of the body shell was taken up with three rows of two individual seats, all with hinged backrests. Those of you old enough can no doubt remember trams and the rat-tat-tat of their wooden seat backs as they were pushed over at the depot to face the opposite direction. The tram could now travel back to town along the same track without having to be turned round, since the driver merely walked round to the other end of the tram where a duplicate set of controls awaited him. Therefore, because of the seats, it became, affectionately, the 'Tram'.

The body was certainly much larger than anything put onto Jowett commercial vehicles in the past. However, in spite of being rather big for the engine size, it did provide us with a complete vehicle with which to prove the chassis technology. And this it certainly did. In fact, being larger and heavier than the intended production model, it more than met the requirements originally laid down. It proved the chassis was most capable of doing the job for which it was intended.

Unfortunately, engine access wasn't as good as it became in the final production body. Nevertheless, we really only wanted something to cover the engine, so the bonnet was little more than a lid – and a rather small one at that – covering the engine compartment.

After all the initial work, the Tram eventually became the department hack and was used both to collect articles for the Experimental Dept. and to run teams of support staff around to race meetings and the like. I vividly remember runs to Silverstone when we were racing and to the Motor Industry Research Association at Nuneaton when we were testing.

Being a rather short engine front to back meant that the gearbox was mounted well forward in the frame. This necessitated an exceptionally long gear lever, which came out of the toe board rather than out of the propshaft tunnel. Because of its length, the gear lever did rather have a tendency to thrash about when the Tram was pulling hard at low revs. However, we overcame this by the time we got to the pilot run of the CD variants. But more of that later.

The old Tram certainly looked smart when it was cleaned up. The paintwork was polychromatic grey and set off this rather large Jowett prototype rather well. You can imagine that, since the body was long, the handling properties left quite a bit to be desired. When it was full of people or goods there was a bit of a tendency for it to sway, necessitating quite a bit of sawing at the steering wheel, especially if there was a bit of a side wind.

However, these were characteristics which were not passed through to the Briggs production-bodied CDs. In fact everything improved when the first Briggs body arrived. It was a duck-egg blue estate car body. A two-door body with side windows and a double rear door opening with windows. Now this really was something.

Part Two

As I said at the end of Part One, everything improved when the first Briggs body arrived. You see, it was built on the production tools and was very smart by the standards of the day. Previously, estate cars had been angular and utility-looking. Not this one. It was nicely proportioned, with a flat bonnet which spread between the fully enclosed front wings – rather reminiscent of the Mk 1 Ford Consul. Some say, in fact, that this was their origin, but I don't really know if that were true. Certainly the grille was very much like that of the Austin A40 Sports of the time, so maybe certain features were taken from a number of contemporary vehicles.

The body was a two-door, each door having easy-drop windows, counter-balanced against levers and springs in the manner of many small commercial vehicles of the day. The windscreen was flat, since curved screens had not yet moved through onto commercial vehicles. The rear load space was accessible through normal double doors, which had a window each. There were also two well-proportioned windows down either side, giving a light and airy interior. You might almost say the body shape was bang up to date, being bulbous and smooth in the style of many of our current cars. Isn't it funny, this time round the shape has originated in Germany.

The instrument panel was centrally mounted between two gloveboxes, or more correctly glove compartments, since there were no lids. The layout comprised the speedometer in the right-hand dial and the various required gauges of the day in the left-hand one. A trafficator switch was above the panel and the starter switch was in the middle of the panel. The handbrake was Javelin/Jupiter-type but mounted on the steering column to the right-hand side. The pedals came up from a floor-mounted pedal box.

There were two unique features of the CD. It was the first car/light commercial to use the 'bottle' combination switch for lights and horn and also the first to use double-dipping headlamps. The bottle switch was mounted on the steering column, just under the steering wheel, and pointed to the offside. It had a rotating switch for side, head and dip where the bottleneck would be, and the bottle 'stopper' was the horn push. Believe me, this was quite an innovation back in the early 1950s. I'll tell you more about the double-dipping headlamps a little later on.

One thing you must remember: there was no heater! Perish the thought! Actually, we did try a ram heater rather half-heartedly for a very short period of time. It didn't work though. It was taken off the top nearside of the radiator core and had a long, wide bore trunking, which led to an elongated canister over the front floorboard. It really was less than useless.

So there we were, with the first production-bodied CD. Ahead of us was a twelve-week continual test programme on a 200-mile route around Yorkshire to be covered every twenty-four hours. The route triangulated on three well-known Yorkshire hills: Greenhow out of Pately Bridge, Kidstone Pass going over from Wharfedale into Wensleydale and Sutton Bank, that notorious climb over the Hambleton Hills between Thirsk and Helmsley. There's a very wicked 1 in 4 hairpin in the middle of it, just when you are groping for revs. The rest of the route was made up of undulating Dales countryside and bends of varying degrees of severity. It was topped off with the only stretch of real straight road in the area, the A1 between Boroughbridge and Leeming Bar. There was an all-night transport cafe at Leeming Bar. Were we glad of it and its open fire?

Oh, I mustn't forget to tell you; in order to load the estate car up to full gross vehicle weight for test purposes, we removed the rear bench seat and fitted two very substantial wooden boxes. In fact we bolted them to the floor running fore and aft. Between them they contained twenty 56lb weights. 10cwts in all! Now we were ready to go.

This particular twelve-week test started at the beginning of February and finished at the end of April. We ran in three shifts and changed over from time to time. The shifts were 7.00 a.m. to 3.00 p.m., 3.00 p.m. to 11.00 p.m. and 11.00 p.m. to 7.00 p.m. It was the night run which was the killer, so it was always shared by two of us. Not surprising either, since it started snowing the second night out and it stayed with us throughout the twelve weeks. You really couldn't be off up the dales in the snow at night on your own; you'd be lost without trace! Don't forget, no snow tyres or chains, only a very chunky nine-horse twin. Think of those three hills! We climbed Sutton Bank in the middle of the night in thick snow with 10cwts onboard. Every night and everyday come to that.

Four of us drove the three shifts. Morning run, Billy Fruin; afternoon, Donald Wade; night run, me and Tommy Laycock. How we ever kept going under those conditions I shall never know. I had oiled wool socks, dispatch riders boots, two pairs of trousers, an enormous heavy coat, balaclava helmet, leather gauntlet gloves with silk inner linings, a flask of coffee laced with rum and I was still frozen! We drove with one hand and wiped the screen with the other – all night. You really have no idea of the severity of this run and yet the CD never missed a beat and never put a foot wrong. In the whole of the twelve weeks we never 'lost it', never had a bump. I must say I was more than impressed.

The handling was first class by the standards of the day. The roadholding steering and brakes all behaved impeccably. However, I did say I would tell you about the double-dipping headlamps, didn't I?

As I said, Tommy Laycock and I started on the night run. We had got through the Dales and been up and down Sutton Bank. We now had the easy, high-speed bit: the run from Boroughbridge to the transport cafe at Leeming Bar. Don't forget that whilst the A1 was straight and fast in this section, it was dual carriageway for only part of the distance in those days. The truckers were travelling down from Scotland overnight – no tachographs then – and they didn't stop for anything. Meeting the first trucker on the single carriageway, we dutifully dipped our lights as he approached us from the north. Suddenly, we realised that he was coming straight for us across the dotted white line in the middle of the road. In order to save our skins we had to take to the grass verge to avoid being hit. But why? What had we done? We got back on course and it happened again with the next trucker, and the next. Then it dawned on us. Until these double-dipping headlamps, the outward sign of a 'dip' was your nearside headlight being extinguished and your offside headlight being pointed down and to the nearside by means of a solenoid activating a hinged reflector. These truckers thought we weren't dipping, so were going to teach us a lesson! What you might call summary jurisdiction. The only thing to do was to explain it to them. So we went into every transport cafe up that section of the A1 and got the lads to come out onto the park and to see that this was the coming thing. Double-dipping headlamps, and please tell your mates!

Having moved onto the afternoon run at one time, I was climbing Sutton Bank when the gear lever came off 'in mi 'and'. Now the gear lever was quite long, since it came out of the toe panel. What had happened was that the weld had broken about 3in out of the gearbox turret. There was no possible way to get it mended where I was so I just had to get back to Bradford. Luckily, I did have a plug spanner with me which was about 6in long and it would fit over the vertical piece of gear lever. However, in order to reach it I had to put my head under the dash. It's a good job there wasn't much traffic about in 1952. I did get back to Idle, but I'm still not quite sure how it came about. One thing for sure, it was a very, very long return leg.

On another occasion, approaching Kidstones Pass, I had a front wheel bearing collapse. I managed to get the CD turned round, but knew I hadn't a hope of effecting a repair. So I set off back to Idle. Now it just so happened that the particular Timken bearing only affected the steering one way. Let's say it was perfectly all right going round left-hand bends, but hell on wheels going round right-handers. I really didn't know where I was going to end up. There was that awful feeling going into a bend of almost 'slack water', do you see what I mean? Again I did make it back, but there were some peculiar excursions on the way.

One of my most amazing friendships came about on this test. It was April now, and we were nearing the end of the run and the snow was not too bad. I had changed onto the morning run and was enjoying the daylight, the sun on the snow and the clear skies. By 9.00 a.m. I had run up Wharfedale and was crossing the saddle to descend into Wensleydale. As I did so, a Meteorological Spitfire flew up Wharfedale, over the saddle and down Wensleydale. I flashed my headlamps and he waggled his wings. We met this way every day for a week. We were the best of friends, and we never knew each other! It's quite extraordinary how the memories are flooding back.

Another view of the CD Estate on test.

Part Three

Here we are with Part Three of my CD memories. It really is quite amazing how all the little interesting instances come flooding back once I put my mind to it and start reflecting upon the days at Idle in the Experimental Department. In fact, before I leave the twelve-week prototype run I told you about in Part Two, there are one or two more episodes worth recalling.

I have told you how we had no chains or snow tyres on the estate car, which by the way was HKW 272. How we still managed to climb the three hills, which triangulated the route, namely Greenhow, Kidstones and Sutton Bank. Well, one night quite early in the test programme, we were approaching Kidstones Pass in a veritable blizzard. I had the wheel and Tommy Laycock was 'watching points'. As we started the climb up Kidstones we soon realised that we could not see ahead for driving snow. It was coming down so heavily that our lights were reflecting back at us. The wipers were not adequately shifting it either. We could not stop and try to reverse because the road was too narrow and there were ditches at both sides which were full of snow. We were, therefore, in a bit of a quandary. So, I dropped the driver's side window and, carefully watching the wall on the offside of the road, gently edged our way towards it as we continued to make forward progress. As we got nearer the wall, I edged away from it and as we got further away from it I edged back towards it. By this method we finally got over the pass. Once we were over and going down into Wenseslydale there was a certain relaxing of tension which, by mutual agreement, necessitated stopping and getting out. The snow was coming down so hard that by the time we had stopped, applied the handbrake, switched off, got out and staggered round

the rear of the CD, the snow had already covered our wheel tracks!

There is another little item worthy of note with regard to the CD's capabilities. Whilst the two hundred-mile route was most definitely a full eight hours of very hard work in early February, it was a totally different story by the time we were into April and the snows were clearing from the roads. I remember being on the morning run in mid-April and actually getting right round the route in under five hours. Now that speaks volumes for the roadholding and suspension of the CD doesn't it? Don't forget the R4 Jupiter chassis was based upon this frame, so it couldn't have been far out could it? It really was very surefooted, and my recollections are of a very safe overall feel to the vehicle. Unlike other vehicles of the time, it was not frisky and it would certainly 'telegraph' you if something was going to happen. As I told you in Part Two, we never lost it over the whole of the twelve weeks, and there were many instances of quite enthusiastically applied motoring going on during that time. We did a couple of rather rapid gyrations one night, between rather high stone walls, but I don't think I should really go into that now. It still makes me go cold!

Right, let's move on now to the other variants within the CD range. There was only one pick-up built, HKY 566, and this was also a very stylish motor for its time. Bear in mind that the CC pick-up was really a 'builders truck' with a stark little cab chopped off behind the door frame and with a plain, flat-vertical cab back. The body was standard wooden drop-side.

The CD cab, on the other hand, housed a bench seat and had rear quarter lights in a very nicely shaped side moulding. Two back lights were in the sloping rear of the cab and there was enough room behind the bench seat for a most useful rear shelf. Instead of a wooden body, the sides continued the same lines as the lower part of the estate car body from the sill downwards. The open load space was finished off with a rather heavy, but very practical, drop-down tailgate. A neatly tailored tonneau cover went over the load area to afford protection to whatever was being carried. The body was green with cream wheels and in the early 1950s it looked extremely stylish. It certainly turned a few heads as it went by.

I took the pick-up down to Dagenham once to the headquarters of Briggs Motor Bodies. I recall I had a spare bench seat in the load space, so obviously discussions were about the bench seat. Being nearly fifty years ago, I have really no idea what was decided that day. However, I do remember that it was a 'there and back' trip from Bradford to Dagenham in the one day. Bradford to Bradford from 8.00 a.m. to 2.00 a.m. next day! And all down the Great North Road as it was then, not even one stretch of dual carriageway. Through each and every town too. It seemed absolutely interminable and I remember singing my heart out somewhere around 1.00 a.m., trying to keep awake!

Now the car, JKU 399, was also a pretty motorcar for its day. Here's a funny thing; all CD windscreens were flat, yet the car had a modern curved backlight. It had quite a cavernous boot, the lines of which followed the rear wing lines. Rather reminiscent of the Morris Oxford of the late 1950s. Not quite as big a car though. However, it would have been very acceptable in those days since it rode and handled every bit as well as the estate car. I recall doing a fast run with it up to Newcastle-on-Tyne and thinking 'This won't half surprise a few Ford, Austin, Morris, etc. owners when it comes out, especially if we make a model with the Javelin engine as a performance saloon'. But more of that later.

What followed next was a full pilot run of vans and estate cars, some nine or ten alto-gether, all off the production jigs at Briggs. These were used to gain more operational experience, so a route was planned for them round the Lake District. There was more main road running on this route than on the Dales route. However, it still included such notorious climbs as Hard Knott, Wrynose and Kirkstone passes. We could never have been accused of mollycoddling our development vehicles. It was during these Lakes tests that we had a rather embarrassing experience. It was a Saturday afternoon and we were coming down Wrynose Pass. Imagine our chagrin to drive through the middle of some motor club's hill climb, trying to come UP Wrynose! We actually got reported in the *Motor Sport* of the time for creating such undignified mayhem.

Sod's Law dictates that the conditions are always at their worst when you are in the most unprotected position. It was decided to gain some more chassis information and so a bare chassis was soon assembled, complete with slave scuttle, dash, steering column and seat. I don't have to spell it out to you who the driver was, do I? By God, it was cold. It rained, it blew, it hailed and now and again it was dry, but always bitterly cold. This test continued for about two to three weeks. I wore a Royal Navy flight deck suit for protection, together with leather helmet and goggles, gauntlet gloves and Wellingtons, and I was frozen! Luckily, a friend of mine owned a farm near Easingwold, so by a circuitous route I usually contrived to call upon him for hot coffee, liberally laced with rum – for medicinal purposes, of course. I well remember breaking a throttle cable on the offside carburettor once, and having acute difficulty in repairing it due to frozen fingers which wouldn't react to what my brain was telling them.

However, to offset such painful memories, I also remember combining business with pleasure and taking one of the CD estates round the Welsh coastline to record some body temperature figures. The weather was glorious, the views magnificent and the CD revelled in it. My wife and I still talk about that week with great affection. Just one of those little cameos.

The most exciting variant of course was the last project we tackled. It was decided to graft a Javelin engine into the original Briggs prototype estate car, HKW 272. This became a most amazing piece of machinery. It had the remote-inclined radiator and thermostatic fan of the R4 Jupiter and I took it to London during the 1953 Earls Court show, where the R4 was first seen by the general public. We were intent upon doing some cooling trials whilst in a highly concentrated metropolitan environment. In order to make some sort of comparison with the standard CD you could liken the difference to that found between the Mk 1 Cortina and the Lotus Cortina, only more so. It went like a scalded rocket, and it had tremendous low-down torque. You remember the extra long central gear stick? When I really poured on the power, the gear lever knob dropped 6in! It could leave Jaguar XK 120's standing off the traffic lights on wooden setts in London – oh yes; wooden sets were still around in plenty in the early 1950s. Talk about a wolf in sheep's clothing. It was absolutely marvellous; I would have given my eye teeth for that motor.

But none of it was to be. What a great shame, what a tremendous amount of potential was killed off in its infancy. I often think about where we could have been by now, had things worked out differently. One thing for sure, you would never get a team like that again and that's a great shame. I still believe the CD could really have been a winner. Just think of it: one basic chassis, four standard bodies – van, estate, saloon and pick-up. A complete Meccano set. Four-cylinder variant for the enthusiasts. What a rally machine that would have made in those days. What a concept, what a waste, what a shame. It nearly worked though, didn't it?

Phill Green, Harrogate, North Yorkshire

[*Phill Green was the Chief Test Driver for Jowett Cars from 1949 to closure in 1954. He now lives in retirement in Harrogate and continues to keep the Jowett name alive in his talks to various Road Transport Groups around the country. He is a member of the Institute of the Motor Industry. I know that Phill did not own the CD, so technically I should not have used this in the book, but it is such an important story, and I really wanted to use it, as many readers will not have heard of the CD range. NS*]

Expensive Habits.

The Jowett hasn't any.

It watches its owner's pocket like America hoarding gold.

It gets the largest possible mileage out of its allowance for petrol, oil and tyres.

(An owner tells us he has got nearly 50,000 miles out of his front tyres and they're still running.)

It refuses to indulge in expensive repair bills.

Its yearly tax is the cheapest in the country.

It is, strange contradiction, generous also —

In the amount of room it provides its occupants, its comfort, the happiness it affords, the enjoyment.

There's nothing a light car will do that the Jowett won't do, a little better.

There's no part on a light car that isn't a little better on a Jowett.

We have the only engine for a light car.

Have a trial free of charge.

Prices from £135.   Tax £7.

JOWETT CARS LTD., IDLE, BRADFORD